Kingdom of Darkness

KINGDOM OF DARKNESS

By F. W. THOMAS

LOGOS INTERNATIONAL
Plainfield, New Jersey

*All Scriptures are quoted from the King James
version of the Holy Bible*

KINGDOM OF DARKNESS
© 1973 by Logos International
Plainfield, N.J. 07060
All Rights Reserved
Printed in the United States of America
Library of Congress Catalog Card Number: 73-75958
ISBN: 0-88270-041-3 (hardcover)
        -034-0 (paperback)

Contents

CONTENTS

Preface

There is an aura of eerie wonderment and mystery surrounding the forbidden occult arts. It is claimed by those who indulge in such things that within the shadowy world of occultism is to be found the true wisdom of the ages. We are told that only a select few have ever really discovered how to climb the transcendental heights to psychic power. Untold numbers have attempted this hazardous climb, but they have not, it is said, been properly instructed; hence, they have fallen on the jagged rocks of defeat and destruction below.

Oriental mysticism has made its way to the West and is now firmly believed and practiced by many. The shrill cry of pagan shamanism is now being heard in our land. Modern would-be gurus are leading multitudes of people into occult bondage with their cryptic utterances and esoteric teachings. What they have to say is usually veiled in arresting language: "Let the ascended spiritual Masters give you the answer to the lonely mystery of man's existence." The courageous and uninhibited are invited to become "explorers of hidden psychic realms."

This hydra-headed thing called "occultism" expresses itself in many forms. The occult is really a study of unfathomable mysteries. Its practices are many and varied, weird and frightening, for they cover the whole field of astrology, fortune-telling, necromancy (consulting the dead), ghosts, hauntings, spiritualism, clairvoyance, spiritual healing, the magic power of charms, white magic, black magic, ESP, witchcraft, sorcery, incubus and succubus (demons who have carnal relations with humans), amulet pacts, Satanism, and the unholy blood pact —selling of one's soul to the devil!

These are but a few of the topics which will be discussed in this book. Certain things said herein will seem mind-boggling and may well strain your credulity. I say this, not to frighten the reader, but rather to prepare him for what lies ahead. I would to God that the dreadful and shocking horrors revealed in these pages were not factual, that they were nothing more than the wild ravings of poor demented minds. But such is not the case.

Our reason for recording these terrifying things is not to cater to the morbid curiosity of sinful men, but to show just how utterly depraved people can become who follow the dark and dangerous path of occultism. The Bible tells us that "God hath made man upright; but they have sought out many inventions" (Eccles. 7:29), and some of them are wicked indeed.

Each new soul coming into our world is born with a potential for greatness and nobility. I am not speaking of materialistic greatness, but spiritual worth and importance! If men would only open up their hearts to the Creator, even as a flower opens its petals to the life-giving rays of the sun, they would become the noble creatures God intended them to be. But instead of seeking after God, most men wish to lead their own lives, independent of any Creator.

There is an old saying that nature abhors a vacuum. Man is born with a capacity and yearning for the supernatural. It is inherent in all of us; man is a supernatural creature by virtue of the fact that he has been created by a supernatural God.

Further, man is destined after death to dwell in a supernatural realm, either heaven or hell. If men will not allow the positive things of God to draw them into a personal relationship with their Creator, then the negative influences will surely attract and bind them. There is no limbo, no "no-man's-land," no middle ground. Jesus said the same thing in these words: "He that is not with me is against me" (Matt. 12:30). When people refuse to follow hard after God, then they develop all sorts of hang-ups and eventually become bound and shackled either by drugs, inordinate lusts, hatred, envy, greed, incontinence, perpetual escape, selfishness, or the sins under discussion in this book—witchcraft and other occult practices.

When one dabbles in occultism, he commits a cardinal sin by breaking the first holy commandment of God: "Thou shalt have no other gods before Me" (Exod. 20:3). To seek help and information from demons, the so-called spirit guides, is a direct violation of God's first law. "And the soul that turneth after such as have familiar spirits, and after wizards, to go a whoring after them, I will even set my face against that soul, and will cut him off from among his people" (Lev. 20:6).

ANSWERING THE CRITICS

The writer fully expects that he will be criticized for exposing the hidden things of darkness. Criticism coming from practicing occultists is to be expected. But some Christians will object and say that it is best to leave the devil and his works alone. Is this head-in-the-sand attitude of "If I don't bother him, maybe he won't bother me" really the proper view for a Christian to hold?

Such persons would have us believe that it is wrong for a Christian to understand the teachings of occultism. They claim that knowledge of occult matters might possibly tempt some inquisitive persons to begin practicing the black arts. Surely they do not believe it wrong for a Christian to speak out against the evils of drug addiction, alcoholism, homosexuality, or any other sin. Untold numbers of human derelicts, bound and shackled by social vices, have been salvaged and brought back to God and respectability because concerned Christians cared enough to tell them about Jesus and His power to save. Surely Christians will not become dope addicts by reading a book that exposes and denounces dope addiction. Nor will they become practitioners of the black arts because they read a book which exposes occultism. It is imperative that we know our Enemy, the better to combat him.

The scripture says, "For we wrestle not against flesh and blood, but against principalities, against powers, against the rulers of the darkness of this world, against spiritual wickedness in high places" (Eph. 6:12). And, "For the weapons of our warfare are not carnal, but mighty through God to the pulling down of strong holds" (II Cor. 10:4). Christians are given yet another admonition: "Lest Satan should get an advantage of us: for we are not ignorant of his devices" (II Cor. 2:11).

In many cases it is ignorance of the devil's works that makes so many Christians ineffective witnesses for Christ. How can Christians intelligently deal with those who are caught up in all kinds of psychic entanglements when they know practically nothing about occultism?

Another criticism some might have is that this book gives place to the devil because it tells about the power of Satan in the lives of people who follow the dark mystical ways of occultism.

One of the things the Bible tells us is that Satan successfully brought about the downfall of Adam and Eve in the Garden of Eden. Would one say that the Bible glorifies Satan because this fact is recorded in God's Word? Holy Writ also mentions that the sorcerers at Pharaoh's court turned their rods into serpents by demonic power. Is the Bible glorifying Satan's power?

In the New Testament we read of one man so possessed with demons that no chain could hold him (Mark 5:1-19). Is this another case of God's Holy Book glorifying the power of demons? What about the devil possessing Judas and causing him to betray Christ?

Many other biblical examples of Satan's workings could be cited. In the same fashion, this book does not glorify what the devil is doing; on the contrary, it exposes his deceptive and beguiling tactics and makes it abundantly clear that there is a far greater power available to any who take Christ as their Savior. For no matter how strong the demon, or how heavy the attack—no matter if the attacker is Satan himself—*Jesus is always victor.*

This spiritual law is never mentioned in any of the how-to books on witchcraft now available in bookstores. They also fail to mention the awful price one has to pay for the use of these forbidden powers. It is intended that this book will set the record straight, that it will enable the concerned Christian to better understand the danger of black magic, sorcery, witchcraft, and other forbidden occult arts, and more effectively minister to those seeking to escape their bondage.

Kingdom of Darkness

1.

The Occult Explosion

■ Never in the history of modern man have so many people shown such interest in pagan occultism. Multitudes today are playing with destructive psychic forces which they do not understand. People from every walk of life are reaching out, seriously trying to make contact with the psychic realm. In the upper echelons of our society can be found government officials, religious leaders, and businessmen who constantly seek help and information from fortune-tellers, astrologers, and spiritualist mediums. Suburban housewives can't wait for the daily newspaper to see what their horoscope has to say. Thousands more are practicing yoga, transcendental meditation, and cosmic consciousness.

An ever-increasing number of teenagers are being drawn into the occult scene. Many of our impressionable youth have an almost uncontrollable desire to experiment with the mysterious. Some begin by dabbling with hypnotism, astrology, ESP, tarot cards, the I Ching and the Ouija board. Once they step through these so-called psychic doors, the promise of greater thrills, wonders, and mystical happenings prompts them to begin investigating the darker aspects of occultism such as witchcraft, black magic, sorcery, and Satanism.

Those who go this route are said to be on the left-hand path and are called *brothers of the shadows*.

Current interest regarding occultism is so great that many high schools and universities now conduct classes in witchcraft and sorcery. These classes are always packed. New York University, for example, had so many people taking their course in Witchcraft, Magic, and Sorcery that regular classrooms could not contain all those interested. The university was forced to hold its classes on witchcraft at one of its largest lecture halls in order to accommodate the overflowing crowds. Schools throughout North America are honeycombed with cells of students practicing occultism. Cyril Chave, head of the English department at Prince of Wales Secondary School, is quoted as saying:

> I have been teaching here [in Vancouver] for better than 25 years and I have seen all the phases the students have passed through: their music, protest, the drug culture.
>
> But from an intellectual point of view, nothing has ever alarmed me so deeply as this perverse fascination for the magical arts. It is everywhere and it could grow with dangerous consequences.[1]

A few short years ago we were stunned to learn that atheistic teachers and parents were successful in getting prayer and Bible reading banned from our schools. On top of this, we have teachers pumping the lie of evolution into young impressionable minds. These denials of our Judeo-Christian heritage have helped to create a fertile field for every foul and imaginable evil plaguing our sick society today—drug abuse, lawlessness, revolution, sexual permissiveness and homosexual practices, and last but not least, the occult craze. God

[1] *Vancouver Sun*, February 2, 1972.

and heaven, the devil and hell have been laughed out the schoolroom window.

The majority of our educators today are still worshiping at the shrine of human reason. In the writer's view, none of the prevailing rationales of intellectualism or humanism can give a satisfactory answer to something outside the physical realm. And when young people, who are naturally inquisitive, start experimenting with occultism, they quickly discover there is something to it. Those who have delved into magical practices testify that things which defied all natural explanation really started happening in their lives. One has told another, and the modern-day occult revival has now burst upon us and is sweeping untold masses of people into a psychic vortex of bondage and doom. If the high priests of science and education had taught students the truth concerning spiritual powers, as found in the Bible, then inquiring young minds would have been better able to properly evaluate the occult sciences.

Occultism has crept into nearly every segment of our society. A large number of department stores are now carrying occult games for children. It is said these "fun" things serve a dual purpose. Not only are they meant to entertain young people, but such games are calculated to make one more sensitive and open to the astral plane.

Even the movie industry is capitalizing on the occult craze. In the last few years, a number of occult films have been shown at theaters across the country, and more are to follow. One box-office hit, *Rosemary's Baby*, even went so far as to glorify a foul incubus demon who copulated with a young man's wife. This was the start of a flood of books, movies, and television programs on black magic, witchcraft, and Satanism.

Books on astrology, witchcraft, and the pursuit of the supernatural are now so numerous that bookstores have special sections for their display. In Vancouver, paperback books on occult subjects are now outselling those on pornography. Binky Marks, of Duthie Books, Ltd., in Vancouver, states, "In the last year and a half, the increase in sales of occult literature has been astounding. The majority of it is being bought by young people, who seem to be looking for a new kind of life. They are buying 79-cent paperbacks, $15 hardcovers, and reprints of 50-year-old titles." [2]

Librarians have told us that books on witchcraft and occultism are the ones most frequently stolen from their shelves, and many libraries now keep their occult books in a special reserved section; if one wishes to borrow a book on this particular subject, he must go to the desk and ask for it. Whenever I have attempted to do so, it turns out to be an exercise in futility, for invariably the book I want is out.

What is the reason for the tremendous surge of occult interest that threatens to engulf our society today? Why do people want to get in league with the dark powers? What prompts them to practice the bizarre rites of sorcery and witchcraft? Is it really happening that in our enlightened age people actually sell their souls to the devil?

Are there really supernatural forces of evil? What happens to persons who contact them? How does fortune-telling work? Is there any danger in astrology, Ouija boards, and fortune-telling? Is there any deliverance from this bondage?

These are some of the questions that will be dealt with in this work.

[2] *Ibid.,* March 3, 1972.

2.

The Two Great Forces

■ If one is to get a true understanding of occultism, he must first understand the nature of man. Within the disquieted soul of man, there is an eternal quest to understand the complex rhythms of his existence. This compulsion to know, is one of the motivating forces in life. Our drive to understand the ultimate meaning of life is a God-given thing, and without this divine current in his make-up, man would become stagnant and would never reach the heights which were intended for him.

Man is not only physical, but he is also spiritual. This is what distinguishes him from the brute creation. The One who created us declared, "Man shall not live by bread alone, but by every word that proceedeth out of the mouth of God" (Matt. 4:4). In view of this scriptural declaration, man cannot really know true peace, happiness, and contentment until he finds God. Within the heart of every person there is a secret chamber that God has made for Himself, and until God fills that inner sanctum of a man's heart with His Presence, there is no rest for the soul.

Some believe that we are helpless creatures caught in an impossible universe, short-lived worms of the dust. How mistaken they are, for man is not only a creature of time but also of eternity. Man has an eternal soul because he is made in the image of an eternal God. Eternity is bound up within the heart of man.

There are two great forces in the universe, good and evil. These two powers differ from each other as light differs from darkness. Good is a beautiful and positive force, whereas evil is negative and ugly. Whence came these two great opposing forces? To answer this question fully would be to solve the riddle of the universe itself.

The Bible tells us that God is the source of all goodness and love. This Supreme Being is the Ineffable Reality, the Divine Architect of the universe, the perfect consummation of all the nobler virtues, who dwells in inexpressible light. He is the one who welded the cosmos together by mighty words of power. This deity of whom we speak is the creator of all things, both visible and invisible, in heaven and earth. It is through the greatness and power of God that man lives and moves and has his being. There is none like unto Him, because He alone is God.

The supreme embodiment of all evil and wickedness is Satan, the devil. He is an intensely malicious personality, vengeful, ruthless, and subtle. Satan is the archenemy of both God and man. He is the great angel of death and darkness. In Hebrew, the name Satan means "adversary."

In Isaiah 14 we are given this account concerning the fall of Lucifer: "How art thou fallen from heaven, O Lucifer, son of the morning! how art thou cast down to the ground, which didst weaken the nations!" Lucifer was originally the greatest archangel in heaven. The name Lucifer means "light bearer." The sight of his own angelic splendor swelled this highest covering cherub with the sin of rebellious pride. Lucifer concluded that his divinely endowed splendor and majesty should entitle him to be equal with Almighty God. The Bible says of Lucifer: "Thou wast perfect in thy ways from the day that thou wast created, till iniquity was found in thee" (Ezek. 28:15).

Lucifer's sin of rebellious pride was an open act of defiance against God. Because of his angelic perfection, his decision to defy God, once made, was irrevocable. The decision was irrevocable, too, for the angels in heaven who followed Satan in his rebellion against God. The Bible gives us a graphic account of Satan's expulsion from heaven:

> *And there was war in heaven. Michael and his angels fought against the dragon, and the dragon fought and his angels. And prevailed not; neither was their place found any more in heaven. And the great dragon was cast out, that old serpent, called the devil and Satan, which deceiveth the whole world: he was cast out into the earth, and his angels were cast out with him.* (Rev. 12:7–9)

When Satan and his rebel angels were cast out of heaven and saw Adam and Eve happy in the Garden of Eden, they became exceedingly jealous and resentful. Satan feared that man, a thing of clay, would gain the Paradise he and his fallen angels had lost. This thought so infuriated Satan that he took possession of a serpent and deliberately tempted Adam and Eve to sin against God. The treachery of the serpent prevailed, and man, God's crowning creation, fell from his state of innocence into sin. Man's relationship with his Creator was severed, and the long dark night of his exile from God began.

Man in his lost and sinful state was not forsaken by God. Instead of obliterating man for his disobedience, God put into operation a plan that will ultimately redeem man and restore him to that state of pristine glory and perfection which was originally his. Lurking in the background, however, is Satan and his host of fallen angels who tenaciously oppose God's plan of salvation for mankind. The devil does everything he can to thwart and frustrate God's great plan of redemption for humanity. All the diabolical powers of hell are marshaled against man to keep him apart from God and in his lost and sinful state. This has ever been the conflict of the ages: God and the devil both have a declared interest in man.

3.

The Kingdom of Darkness

■ The most harrowing fact in the universe is that the kingdom of darkness exists. Many so-called intellectuals consider it utter madness to believe in the reality of Satan and his demons. Men who are educated beyond their intelligence just cannot bring themselves to believe that there is something in the universe incomprehensible to them.

But Satan and his wicked cohorts do exist. Christ makes this fact unshakably clear in Matt. 12:26, where our Lord tells us that Satan does have a kingdom: "And if Satan cast out Satan, he is divided against himself; how shall then his *kingdom* stand?"

The term "kingdom" suggests order, rule, and authority. Satan's kingdom consists of a hierarchy of principalities and powers, fallen angels of various ranks, each with legions of demons at his command. And above all the fallen angels and demons stands his Satanic majesty, the prince of devils!

This government of evil dwells in mid-heaven. From various thrones, the devil's angels exercise their Satanic rule over the whole earth. There is a constant rivalry among the evil angels for greater power. Those of higher rank in the kingdom of Satan maintain their respective positions, not by con-

11

sent of the lower orders of fallen angels, but solely through
greater fierceness and power.

DEMONS

Fallen angels are constantly dispatching delegations of
demons to various places on earth in order to strengthen the
evil forces at work in our world. Demons are spirits who seek
to possess people in order to gratify their insatiable, perverted lusts. These dark fiends are forever enticing mortals to
break the holy laws of God. They tenaciously withstand the
forces of righteousness at work on the earth.

The great schools of magic teach that all knowledge and
power can be obtained by communicating with demons.
Demons are said to be very skillful in the abstract sciences, in
languages of both man and beast, in theology, philosophy,
history, magic, sorcery, and prophecy. They can control the
elements of both wind and water, and even influence the passions of men's minds.

Demons are divided into many classes, kingdoms, and
principalities. Demonologists maintain that there are devil
dukes, devil marquises, devil earls, devil counts, devil
knights, devil presidents, and devil prelates. These constitute
what is known as the Infernal Government Order. They are
the routed forces of Lucifer who have organized themselves
to oppose the true and living God.

Down through the ages, sorcerers and black magicians
have attempted to get in league with demons of higher rank
because the higher-ranking demons are able to bestow
greater favors than those of a lower order. Sorcerers and warlocks have their "unholy books," just as Christians have their
Holy Bible, and their demonic manuals tell us much concerning demons and their activities.

The great occult masters usually kept records of their conjuring experiences with spirits. Arch-necromancers would utter dreadful incantations and go through indescribable profanities in order to conjure up a demon of power. For centuries these unholy rites were passed on orally from one generation to the next. Some who dared to invoke the infernal forces wrote down their experiences and rites in manuscript form which they zealously guarded. Such books are known in black magic circles as *The Grimoires*. These once-secret writings of sorcerers contain much information concerning demons. Here are but a few of the demons mentioned, along with some of their characteristics:

ABIGOR: A grand duke of hades. He often appears as a knight bearing lance and standard. Sorcerers claim that he is a demon of the superior order who is able to foretell the future, especially in matters pertaining to war. sixty of the infernal legions are under his command.

ADRAMELECH: Chancellor of the infernal regions. This particular demon was worshiped in ancient Assyria, and children were burned to death on altars erected to Adramelech. The ancient rabbis tell us that he often appears either in the likeness of a mule or peacock.

ALASTOR: A very cruel demon, the "chief executioner to the monarch of hell." He fills the post of Nemesis— agent of retribution and vengeance.

ALDINACH: A demon worshiped by the ancient Egyptians. He has power over the elements and can stir them up against the unwary traveler, causing tempests, hurricanes, earthquakes, hailstorms, and rainstorms. Sorcerers claim that they have often conjured up this demon to sink ships at sea. When successfully evoked, he takes the shape of a woman.

ALOCER: One of the grand dukes of hades and said to be a demon of great power. When conjured up, he appears in the form of a medieval knight mounted on an enormous horse. His face is like that of a lion with a fiery red complexion and burning eyes. He teaches astronomy and the liberal arts to those who serve him. Thirty-six legions of devils are under his command.

AMDUSCIAS: Another of the grand dukes of hades. When evoked, he takes the form of a unicorn. He has the power to give concerts and can make you hear the playing of musical instruments. Those who have had this experience swear that they heard the music, but could see nothing!

AMON: A great and powerful marquis demon who inhabits hades. When evoked, he appears as a wolf with a serpent's tail, vomiting fire.

AMY: Grand President of Hades, and one of the chief princes of the infernal empire. He often appears in a human form, enveloped with flames. Thirty-six of the infernal legions are under his command.

ANNEBERG: An intensely wicked and fearsome demon who haunts certain mines in Europe. He appears in the form of a horse, with a huge neck and terrifying burning eyes.

ASMODEUS: A demon of lust and the personification of rage. When conjured up, he has three heads: those of a bull, a man, and a ram. Madame de Montespan, mistress of Louis XIV, sacrificed children to Asmodeus in 1673 to secure her hold on the king's affection by black magic.[1]

AZIABEL: A demon prince of the water and mountain spir-

---

[1] Collin de Plancy, *Dictionnaire Infernal*, 1863.

its. Those who have conjured him up report that he appears wearing a large crown of pearls.

BAAL: A mighty spirit king who rules over sixty-six legions of infernal spirits. Sorcerers who have conjured him up report that he appears in divers shapes, sometimes taking the form of a toad, sometimes that of a cat, sometimes that of a man, and sometimes he even appears in all three forms at once. He speaks in bellowing hoarse tones and demands homage before giving service.

BELIAL: This name is mentioned on a number of occasions in Holy Scripture (Deut. 13:13; Judges 19:22; I Kings 21:10–13; II Chron. 13:7). "What concord hath Christ with Belial?" (II Cor. 6:15). Belial is said to be a powerful demon king who was created next after Lucifer. He appears in the likeness of an angel in a chariot of fire. He speaks with a pleasant voice and will declare that of all among the higher-ranking spirits he fell first. His office is to distribute presentations and rank to those in the infernal realm who have pleased Satan. He gives familiars to sorcerers and witches. Some fifty legions of fallen spirits are under his authority. Sorcerers are warned that King Belial must have offerings, gifts, and blood sacrifices before he will meet any demands. The name Belial means extreme wickedness and destruction and hopeless ruin.

BOTIS: A great demon earl who rules over sixty legions of spirits. When he makes his appearance, it is in the form of an ugly viper; then at the command of the sorcerers, he puts on human shape with large fierce-looking teeth and two horns. He holds a large sharp sword in his hand and can tell things past and things to come.

Many ancient civilizations have left numerous records de-

scribing the forms of evil spirits. The Babylonians speak of
demons appearing with bodies of dogs and paws of lions,
eagle legs and scorpion-like tails, having human skulls for
heads with protruding horns and bat-like wings. And Holy
Scripture supports the view that demons can appear in very
grotesque forms. In the ninth chapter of Revelation, the
apostle John describes the locust-like demons loosed from
the Pit in the end time:

> And the shapes of the locusts were like unto horses prepared
> unto battle; and on their heads were, as it were, crowns like gold,
> and their faces were as the faces of men. And they had hair as
> the hair of women, and their teeth were as the teeth of lions. And
> they had breastplates, as it were breastplates of iron; and the
> sound of their wings was as the sound of chariots of many horses
> running to battle. And they had tails like unto scorpions, and
> there were stings in their tails: and their power was to hurt men
> five months. And they had a king over them, which is the angel
> of the bottomless pit, whose name in the Hebrew tongue is
> Abaddon.

On another occasion, John declares, "And I saw three unclean spirits like frogs come out of the mouth of the dragon,
and out of the mouth of the beast, and out of the mouth of
the false prophet. For they are the spirits of devils, working
miracles, which go forth unto the kings of the earth and of
the whole world" (Rev. 16:13-14).

In heathen lands, men have attempted to reproduce the
likeness of demons in idol form. H. A. Baker, a missionary to
pre-Communist China for many years, tells us:

> All over China, "hell temples" depict in gruesome horror what
> the wicked in hell suffer, tormented by devils, each in accord
> with his own misdeeds. Each wrong-doer is represented as being

punished by devils with the extreme retribution his particular sin brought: the murderer being slowly murdered, the covetous being fed fiery gold, and the cruel being treated like brutes.

Every Chinese who knows about these hell temples will tell you that the idols in the temples are images of what a certain emperor saw when led in spirit to see the realities of the underworld. The heathen and pagan from prehistoric times believed in hell, not because they imagined it, but because they had been allowed to see it.[2]

Testimonies are on record that people have seen demons as "high as a door," with ugly-shaped chins and warty heads. Others speak of seeing demons with bulging eyes, or eyes like a serpent. The bodies of some demons are just as grotesque and ugly as their faces. Some have scale-like bodies and serpent's eyes. There are demons only two or three feet high, and these dwarf-like creatures usually follow the larger ones around.

The Bible tells us about the "hairy seirim," translated as *devils* or *satyrs*. According to the Old Testament, these were "goat-like demons" (Lev. 17:7; II Chron. 11:15). Some maintain they have seen bat-like demons, dog-like demons, and cat-like demons. The Bible also speaks of certain demons called "familiar spirits." These are the evil spirits who impersonate the dead. In a seance, familiar spirits, claiming to be the departed dead, speak through a medium. Spirits using the medium's vocal cords are often able to mimic the voice characteristic of some departed loved one.

Demons have appeared in the form of a woman, a man, a small boy or girl, or even as an angel of light. There are some demons who like to wear gaudy-colored apparel. In the demonic manuals, sorcerers relate they have seen an infernal-

[2] *Plains of Glory and Gloom*, p. 155.

looking demon duke clad from head to foot in crimson raiment, gloriously crowned, and surrounded by flames while bestriding a crocodile, and in his right hand carrying a hissing viper.

Then there is a lower order of demons who prefer to appear in dirty rags and filthy garments. Many individuals connected with the hard-line drug culture have an irresistible urge to wear gaudy apparel and seem absolutely obsessed with wearing dirty clothes and maintaining a filthy appearance. Could it be that demons are actually obsessing and even possessing many of these people?

THE TERRIFYING INCUBUS

In all of occultism, nothing is more weird than the incubus (male) and succubus (female) demons. These spirit entities are demons of lust who take on either male or female form so they can sexually molest their victims. If the much disputed scriptural passage of Genesis 6:1–6 is taken in a literal sense, then cohabitation between evil spirits and humans is a distinct possibility. Many Bible scholars believe that when the world was young, God incarcerated a number of fallen angels in the lowest pits of hell for this sin:

> And the angels which kept not their first estate, but left their own habitation, he hath reserved in everlasting chains under darkness unto the judgment of the great day. (Jude 6)

The history of early civilization tells us of the dreaded night-nymph, who would entice Babylonian and Assyrian travelers into having carnal relations with them. Upon yielding to the demands of these hauntingly seductive night-maidens, men would become possessed and were driven insane.

Certain modern-day occultists still advocate that for greater psychic power one should open oneself sexually to the astral masters. Dion Fortune, who was a very knowledgeable occultist, states that one well-known psychic advises his women disciples that "they should not live with their husbands, but allow themselves to be put in touch with an astral lover." "Not only does this precious advice break up homes," says Dion Fortune, "but in several cases, to my personal knowledge, it has rendered the recipients mentally unbalanced." [3]

In his *Compendium Maleficarum* (1608), the scholarly Guazzo states, "The incubus can assume either a male or a female shape; sometimes he appears as a full-grown man, sometimes as a satyr, and if it is a woman who has been received as a witch, he generally assumes the form of a rank goat."

A satyr is a creature part human and part he-goat. Such creatures have been known to materialize at a witch's sabbath and are noted for their lasciviousness and riotous conduct. The term *satyriasis* is used in psychiatry to denote "a morbid and uncontrollable sexual desire in men." The demon fiend called a satyr is mentioned twice by Isaiah the prophet (Isa. 13:21; 34:14). In both instances, satyr demons are referred to in connection with the destruction of Babylon and Edom.

Here is but a portion of the judgment leveled against Babylon: "It shall never be inhabited. . . . But wild beasts of the desert shall lie there; and their houses shall be full of doleful creatures; and owls shall dwell there, *and satyrs shall dance there*" (Isa. 13:20–21).

In his excellent book *The Bible; Its Christ, and Modernism,*

[3] Dion Fortune [pseud], *Sane Occultism* (London; Rider, 1929), p. 128.

T. J. McCrossan introduces us to Dr. Cyrus Hamlin, of Robert College, Constantinople. One day this learned Christian was challenged by a Turkish colonel to show him just one real proof that the Bible was truly divinely inspired. Dr. Hamlin asked the colonel if he had ever visited the ruins of ancient Babylon. The colonel replied that he had indeed been there and then proceeded to tell the following story:

A rich sheikh and bearers had been hired by the colonel and his party to take them hunting at the ruins of Babylon. Upon their arrival, they found many wild animals, owls, and birds dwelling in the ancient ruins. "In fact," said the colonel, "we had the best hunting of our lives." What annoyed the colonel and his party was that they had to go miles away from the ruins at night to pitch their tent. Vainly they tried to bribe the sheikh and his men to camp right there at the ruins of Babylon, but they flatly refused, saying, "that no Arab had even been known to camp there, because it was haunted after dark by all manner of evil spirits, who would surely kill them or bring great evil upon them." Dr. Hamlin then opened his Bible and asked the colonel to read the previously quoted passage.

This remarkable fulfilled prophecy of Scripture convinced the Turkish colonel that the Bible is God's Book.

DEMONS AND IDOL-WORSHIP

Many people scoff at the idea of taking heathen idol-worship seriously. But from early Christian writers of the Roman period, we know that the heathen often heard voices coming out of their idols. Those who have made a study of such things tell us that evil spirits often take up their abode in these idols, and on numerous occasions could clearly be heard to speak from within them. It is understandable why even some of the highly educated heathen worshiped statues and gave offerings to these idols as though they were gods.

In an excellent booklet put out by Moody Press, the incident is told of a certain well-educated teacher who went into a Hindu temple. Just for the fun of it, this brash intellectual "took the holy ashes of the temple and used them to clean his teeth." The account tells us that he went insane. The possessed man was then brought to a respected Christian leader who prayed for him. We are told that the man was indeed delivered, but since he refused to give his heart to Christ, he was re-possessed and driven to insanity again.[4]

In another instance, a woman in India broke an idol. She did this out of enthusiasm for the Christian religion. However, when the woman smashed the Hindu idol, she immediately became possessed. Upon being brought into the Christian church for prayer, the demon cried out, "She broke my idol. That is why I possessed her." The evil spirit was cast out. But since this woman does not live an overcoming Christian life, the devil sometimes returns.[5]

Intellectualism is no safeguard against demon possession. The Creator has endowed man with a built-in immunity against demonic intrusion. There is no door that can be opened from the outside which leads to the citadel of man's soul. The latch is on the inside, and only man has the power to open it. Each one of us has been given the right of free choice; we can open our hearts to either God or Satan. If we live just to satisfy the carnal desires of the flesh, then we are the servants of sin. The more a person yields to fleshy temptations, the less he is able to resist sin's downward pull. A person who chooses this way of life quickly finds out that he

---

[4] *Demon Experiences in Many Lands* (Chicago, Ill.: Moody, 1960), p. 23.
[5] *Ibid.,* p. 23.

has developed an unnatural appetite for unbridled lust and carnality. His whole being now cries out to satisfy that thing burning within him.

Each time a person seeks to gratify the ever-growing un-natural vice which has gripped him, whether it is alcoholism, gluttony, dope addiction, illicit sex, or homosexuality, he finds that his sinful habit becomes more demanding than it was previously. The victims of vice are caught in a vicious circle. They have opened their heart's door to him who is the author of sin, Satan the devil. Once a person becomes bound in this manner, then the devil has a right to possess that soul until such time as a stronger power is invoked to drive him out.

4.

Firsthand Experience

■ From my own experience, I know all too well that the testimonies of others who have seen the fiends of darkness are valid.

As a boy of six, I had a supernatural experience which I shall never forget. One night while I was lying awake in bed, a large, evil-looking, black face appeared at my bedroom window. How could someone be standing outside my second-story bedroom window looking at me when there was nothing for him to stand on? I recall crawling down to the foot of my bed so that I might get a better look at this strange sight. Sure enough, the face was really there!

Almost simultaneously, there appeared beside my bed a dwarf-like creature with a devil's head. This thing was about three feet tall and had a weird, oversize head with large ugly warts all over his red glowing face. Somehow I knew that the unearthly creature standing before me was the devil. During this eerie experience, I was more puzzled than afraid. How could the devil be so small?

While I was staring in wonderment at this imp from the nether regions, a voice that seemed to come from right alongside me spoke the following words three times: "Look at this thing and never forget it."

The next eleven years passed with no further demonic visitations. Then, early one April morning, when I was seventeen years old, three loud knocks came right over the headrest of my bed. These knocks were so loud and forceful that my grandmother in the next bedroom also clearly heard them. That same night, I fell from the roof of my grandmother's house, which was a three-story building, to the hard pavement below. In this fall, my back was broken in three places, both feet sustained compound fractures, and there were also other injuries. The doctors were fearful that perhaps I might never walk again.

One night, several weeks before the accident, I had casually picked up a Bible in my grandmother's house and started to read at random from the Book of Revelation. The Bible had always been rather dull and uninteresting to me. But on this occasion, everything was different; the pages seemed to come alive. Events connected with the end of our world, the battle of the great day of God Almighty, the vials of God's wrath being poured out upon this wicked world, and locust-like demons coming up from the bottomless pit having lion's teeth and faces of men held me spellbound with fear and awe.

The drama of the ages seemed to unfold before my eyes. The reason for man's existence was beginning to make sense. A whole new dimension was opening up for me. In my reading of the Bible that night, I found myself strangely drawn to the rider on the white horse mentioned in the Apocalypse, whose eyes are said to be *like a flame of fire*. This is the One of whom it is written:

And he was clothed with a vesture dipped in blood: and his name is called The Word of God. And the armies which were in heaven followed him upon white horses, clothed in fine linen, white and clean. And out of his mouth goeth a sharp sword, that with it he should smite the nations: and he shall rule them with a rod of iron: and he treadeth the winepress of the fierceness and wrath of Almighty God. And He hath on his vesture and on his thigh a name written, KING OF KINGS AND LORD OF LORDS. (Rev. 19:13–16)

As I lay in the hospital, the cords of God's love were tugging at my heart, but discouraging thoughts started to haunt me day and night. Would I ever walk again? Would I remain permanently paralyzed? Would my life be spent confined in a wheelchair? How would I ever earn a living? Oh God, why had this happened to me? After several operations and much excruciating pain, I was sent home from the hospital, unable to walk. God in His goodness, however, allowed me to get well and strong again. Praise be to His blessed name.

That following winter, after recuperating from this accident, I had the most frightening experience of my life. I hesitate to talk or write of it, but it is not my intention to write about the occult merely from a theoretical point of view. The author is not one who deals with supernaturalism from an armchair position; he has had both positive and negative spiritual experiences.

One cold winter's night in Eastern Canada, I was making my way home from a friend's place, where we had been talking until two o'clock in the morning. The ground was covered with fresh-fallen snow, and everything was quiet save for the whining of a cold midwinter's wind. To make my way home required the walking of three blocks. The street was deserted, the light snow still unbroken. Suddenly, I was stopped in my tracks by clearly and distinctly spoken words: "Stop! Go home the other way, for there is something at the corner of this street that will greatly frighten you."

I did stop and give consideration to this forceful message, but shrugged it off, saying to myself that if there was anyone waiting for me at the end of the street, I would deal with him. Pulling my overcoat a little tighter around me, and putting my head down to break the force of the wind, I continued walking.

Just as I approached the corner, there loomed up before me the biggest man—if you could call him a man—I had ever seen. I would estimate that he was between seven and eight feet tall, standing directly in front of me and blocking my path.

The presence of this large man dressed in black was so frightening that I did not dare look up into his face. Never in all my life have I known such a cold paralyzing fear. My heart started to thump so wildly that I thought it would burst.

After a long moment of excruciating silence, this person spoke in a very commanding voice: "Give me a quarter!" Reaching into my pocket, I quickly pulled out all my money —one twenty-five-cent piece! I dropped the coin into the out-stretched hand. When his hand had closed around it, suddenly this strange person vanished before my very eyes. I remember saying to myself, "Am I going mad?" Looking down into the snow, I realized the only footprints that could be seen were my own!

One can only speculate as to the reason for such an encounter. Perhaps the devil was trying to impress on me the fact that even though I was seeking God, he still had dominion over me. And God Himself might have permitted this harassment to establish once and forever in my mind, the absolute reality of Satan's kingdom. Be that as it may, it is not all that uncommon for demons to appear and demand offerings from people. Such a thing has been known to happen on different occasions, expecially in heathen countries. In regard to such unusual occurences, it is well to heed the following words spoken by Saint Paul: "For now we see through a glass, darkly: but then face to face: now I know in part; but then shall I know even as also I am known" (I Cor. 13:12). The full meaning of such weird experiences will be made clear only in eternity.

The incident did one thing: It put a real hunger in my heart to know God, even as the prophets and apostles of old knew Him. I could no longer be satisfied with merely a creedal knowledge; the desire to know God in a very real and personal way became the consuming passion of my life. It was not long after the crossroad experience that God gloriously saved me and filled me with His blessed Holy Spirit.

It is essential to remember that in order for Christians to be effective in dealing with the souls of men, they must have the power of God in their lives. It is particularly important that Christians be filled with and empowered by the Holy Spirit if they are to win those who are held in bondage by the powers of darkness. Neither psychiatry nor medicine can cure occult oppression. Only the power of the Living God can set the captives free. "For this purpose the Son of God was manifested, that he might destroy the works of the devil" (I John 3:8).

When Christ ascended to heaven, He commissioned the Church to carry out a ministry of witnessing and deliverance. The last words our Lord spoke before returning to His Father had to do with the matter of witnessing: "But ye shall receive power after that the Holy Ghost is come upon you: and ye shall be witnesses unto me—" (Acts 1:8). Those of us who have received the power of God in our lives are duty-bound to fulfill the divine commission.

The writer has conversed with a number of spiritualist mediums and other occult practitioners. Those who are deeply involved claim to have a special spirit guide. It is interesting to note how Satan imitates the workings of God. In John 14:15–17 our Lord gives the following promise:

> If ye love me, keep my commandments. And I will pray the Father, and he shall give you another Comforter, that he may abide with you for ever. Even the Spirit of truth; whom the world cannot receive, because it seeth him not, neither knoweth him: but ye know him; for he dwelleth with you, and shall be in you.

The believer in Christ is promised a "Comforter," One whom Jesus calls "the Spirit of truth." He tells us that the Holy Spirit will not only be *with* each believer but also *in* him. Just as each born-again Christian is indwelt by the blessed Holy Spirit, so every genuine medium, fortune-teller, astrologer, witch, sorcerer, and black magician is indwelt by *an unholy spirit*.

5.

Under Attack

■ Every individual can be likened to a fortress. Surely all of us are aware that Satan has declared war on humanity. Our adversary, the devil, stands back and carefully studies each human being on earth even as a commander in wartime thoughtfully outlines the strategy he will use to take a certain fortress. Every weak area must be known so that the military commander might know where best to attack.

The commander in chief of hell, who is a master strategist, does likewise. He looks for the weakest area in your life and mine, and when this has been determined, demonic legions are sent to attack us at that point. If the invading demons can break through a person's spiritual defenses, they can seize and take control of that particular area in one's life. Once these evil spirits have established a beachhead, either in the body or mind, they move on, waging warfare in other areas of a person's life until the whole personality is infiltrated, blitzed, and occupied by demonic influence. The emissaries of Satan have one mission: to break down and destroy the occupant of the human fortress—man's immortal soul.

Only one who has been delivered from demon possession or Satanic attack can really appreciate this dimension of

God's mercy and power. There are no words that can describe the awful fear of actually beholding horrid demon fiends who have come to attack and rend you.

CHRISTIANS AND DEMONIC ATTACK

Many times we tend to think that a person must be terribly sinful if he is attacked by demons, but there are numerous cases on record where very godly Christians have come under direct demon attack. The more a Christian lives the right kind of life, the greater threat to Satan he becomes. In fury, Satan may launch an onslaught, but the Lord will always bring the Christian through the ordeal, and paradoxically, he will be the stronger and more useful in the Lord's service because of it.

The following story was told to me by a fine Christian couple whom I have known for years. When the woman who related the incident to me was a young girl, she lived on the outskirts of Winnipeg with her parents. The woman's mother was a devout Christian who really loved God. One Sunday night all the older members of the family were at church except the mother, who had stayed home to look after the small children. As the mother was doing her chores that night, suddenly loud supernatural knockings could be heard coming from the corner of a room. The woman spoke out angrily: "Knock, you old devil! Knock! You can't hurt me; I'm in the Lord's hands!" Immediately some unseen presence seized the mother and started choking her. In desperation she cried unto the Lord for deliverance. Release from the demonic attack did not come instantly. As the woman continued to call upon God for help, other members of the family arrived home from church. Upon seeing what was happening, they banded together and rebuked the foul force in the name of our Lord Jesus Christ. The demonic grip around the woman's neck was broken.

It should be mentioned that the mother had been trying to win the family next door to the Lord. There was much opposition because the father of that unsaved household was an extremely wicked person who opposed her every effort. The daughter states that her mother learned a real lesson from this experience. Instead of reverently using the Lord's name to rebuke Satan, she had, in a careless manner, frivolously rebuffed the Evil One in her own strength and was overcome. She learned by bitter experience what the archangel Michael knew:

> Yet Michael the archangel, when contending with the devil he disputed about the body of Moses, durst not bring against him a railing accusation, but said, *The Lord rebuke thee.* (Jude 9)

When Christians are involved in a conflict with demonic forces, they should be exceedingly diligent, sober-minded, and above all prayerful. It is true that God has given Spirit-filled Christians authority over the devil and his dark powers. Such authority, however, can be properly exercised only when one is in right relationship with God. If there is unconfessed sin or backsliding in a Christian's life, the devil can give that person a bad mauling and will often gain the upper hand during times of real spiritual encounter. It is always wise to ask God's forgiveness and full protection before engaging in spiritual combat.

In his booklet, *Begone Satan*, a Catholic pastor relates that he was asked to go and pray for a poor demon-possessed woman. Upon arriving at the parish and seeing the woman's frightful condition, he requested that some men be picked to come and hold the raging woman while prayer was being made for her. Several of the biggest and strongest men volunteered for the job. These men did their job well and held the demonic woman secure during the rite of exorcism, but midway through the solemn prayer of expulsion, the demons spoke through their victim and started revealing the secret unconfessed sins of those men who were holding their prize. Pandemonium broke out! Many people present were greatly embarrassed. The good priest suggests that in future cases it would be far better to have only the most spiritual take part in such undertakings.

A solemn warning is given in Holy Scripture: "Be sober, be vigilant; because your adversary the devil, as a roaring lion, walketh about, seeking whom he may devour" (I Pet. 5:8). This admonition of Scripture is given to Christians. Saint Paul is clearly stating here that if children of God are not sober, watchful, and vigilant, Satan can devour them. There are instances in the Bible where such a thing happened.

Paul speaks of "Hymenaeus and Alexander; whom I have delivered unto Satan, that they may learn not to blaspheme" (I Tim. 1:20).

When God has exhausted every avenue of approach to the sinning Christian, and he still refuses to yield to the gentle wooings of Holy Ghost conviction, then God has been known to permit Satan to have his way with him, "for the destruction of the flesh, that the spirit may be saved" (I Cor. 5:5). May none of us ever have to experience this extreme chastening from the Lord God! The Bible declares, "It is a fearful thing to fall into the hands of the living God" (Heb. 10:31).

Demons cannot attack Christians unless God grants them permission to do so. When this does occur, it is usually allowed for chastisement. Then again, it may be that God wants to teach His child advanced lessons in spiritual warfare, as in the case of Job. You will recall that Satan wanted to attack Job and destroy him. However, the Bible informs us that Satan could not touch Job because God had placed a protective hedge around His servant. It was only when God granted the devil special permission to test Job that he could be attacked, and then only to a limited extent. Holy Scripture tells us that Job kept his faith and integrity in God and thus came through the sustained Satanic attack, not only victorious, but tempered and stronger than ever.

Demonic attacks can also happen to people who flagrantly and repeatedly break the holy commandments of God. Jesus warned one man whom He had healed of an infirmity, "Behold, thou art made whole: sin no more, lest a worse thing come unto thee" (John 5:14). What is this "worse thing"? I believe the answer was given by Christ when He uttered these startling words:

> When the unclean spirit is gone out of a man, he walketh through dry places, seeking rest, and findeth none. Then he saith, I will return into my house from whence I came out; and when he is come, he findeth it empty, swept, and garnished. Then goeth he, and taketh with himself seven other spirits more wicked than himself, and they enter in and dwell there; and the last state of that man is worse than the first. (Matt. 12:43–45)

OCCULTISM AND DEMONIC ATTACKS

Another way people can become demon-oppressed and even demon-possessed is by dabbling in occultism. The Scriptures teach that God has set certain laws and boundaries which man must not transgress. Any unlawful trafficking in the occult often brings an immediate punishment. Case histories show that those who practice the occult arts are often troubled at night by spook phenomena. Untold numbers of people have had nervous breakdowns as a result of occult activities, and involvement with the cults.

And as I am writing these words, I am listening to a religious program called "Harvest Time." A young man has given his testimony of how he was delivered from an unhealthy interest in ESP and other occult practices. In the interview, this young man, an undergraduate at Indiana University, tells how he and fourteen other students had gathered at his apartment one night to find out the real source of ESP power. They drew a magic circle and called upon the name of Beelzebub.* After a short time, an eerie orange glow appeared over the leader's head. Staring at them from the midst of this strange orange glow was the specter of a hideous face, with slits for eyes and horns on its head. When this diabolical manifestation of evil burst into a spasm of maniacal laughter, the students ran shrieking from the apartment. One girl in her fright cried out, "Oh, Jesus! Oh, Jesus!" Immediately the demon vanished. Later, the leader of the group was converted to Christ and is now filled with the Holy Spirit.

In his book, *The Haunted Mind*, Dr. Nandor Fodor relates that a certain London woman had an ardent interest in demonology. She was filled with an obsessive curiosity about the devil and wanted to know more about him. She persuaded a young lad who was living at her home to be her hypnotic subject. On six different occasions, she hypnotized him and ordered him to bring up the devil from hell. While under hypnosis, the boy would thrash around crying that he was afraid. The fanatical woman was so intent on conjuring up the devil that she paid no heed to the boy's pitiful cries.

* The Lord of the flies.

Finally, on the sixth try, a strange light appeared in the magic circle, and then out of that misty haze two dreadful bulging eyes materialized that gorgonized her from head to foot with a penetrating stare. With the blood running cold in her veins, this woman somehow managed to summon her remaining courage and haltingly asked, "Who are you?" The hypnotized boy answered in a voice that had a distinct hissing tone to it, "I am the Evil that you wanted conjured up."

The whole room was icy cold, and a putrid stench filled the air. Dr. Fodor tells us that the woman shrieked, "go back! Go back from whence you came. Never appear again! I do not want you!" With a rumbling rushing sound, the light in the magic circle disappeared.

It took many days before she and the boy recuperated from the terrifying experience. It is reported that on five different occasions, this same evil force has tried to gain control of the boy again.

Jehovah's Witnesses and Demonic Attacks

Evil spirits have an exceeding hatred for the blood of Christ, as Christian workers who have dealt with demon-possessed people can readily testify.

Some years ago I was asked by my good friend, Nick Krushnisky (missionary to Taiwan, Free China, for some thirteen years), to come and assist him in dealing with two Jehovah's Witnesses. During our discussion, it became apparent that the two articulate young men of *Watchtower* persuasion were not going to be moved by scriptural argument. They had been indoctrinated to such an extent that it was virtually impossible to reason with them.

These two dead-eyed Jehovah's Witnesses were trying to prove that all church people were deceived and under Satan's control. My friend and I attempted to show from Holy Scripture that actually the Witnesses were the ones being misled. The debate raged for some two hours. Time after time they flatly refused to admit the truth of God's Word. The whole discussion seemed an exercise in futility.

Finally, I gave up talking and started praying while my friend continued to act as spokesman for the Christian position. Suddenly I was prompted to ask one of the JWs, "Mister, if one really and truly belongs to Christ, then he should be able to sincerely say from his heart that the blood of Jesus Christ, God's Son, has cleansed *me* from all sin."

"Oh, I can say that," stated the JW.

"Then do so, and we'll accept that you are Christians," was our reply.

The Witness started hedging then, and it was only after much prompting that he finally consented to repeat the statement.

In a strong clear tone, the JW attempted to say, "The blood of Jesus Christ, God's Son, has clea-rrr—" He was unable to finish this declaration of faith! Furthermore, the JW had fallen out of his seat and was now staggering like a drunken man, desperately trying to break free from some unseen force that was choking him. The other JW went to assist his comrade, and both fled from the building.[1]

What shall we say concerning the JW who was choked by an unseen power? It should be pointed out that he really considered himself to be a true Christian; in fact, JWs regard themselves as the only true people of God on earth today. Consequently, he no doubt reasons that if anyone could say, "The blood of Jesus Christ, God's Son, has cleansed *me* from

---

[1] The writer has had many dealings with Jehovah's Witnesses. See the author's book, *Masters of Deception* (Grand Rapids, Mich.: Baker Books,) for help in dealing with such false teachers.

all sin," certainly it should be one of Jehovah's Witnesses! What a frightening way to discover who is really lord and master of one's life!

The author has in his files a number of letters from former Jehovah's Witnesses who have come under direct demonic attack since leaving the Watchtower Society. One woman was an ardent JW for many years. Upon reading literature put out by another religious group, she became aware that the Witnesses were doctrinally in error.

Her attempts to share her newfound ideas with JW friends and family members incurred the wrath of Satan. After a heated discussion one night with her JW brother and his wife, the woman went to bed. No sooner had she lain dow than her limbs were paralyzed by strange electrical current. The atmosphere in her bedroom became charged with an awful evil presence. Suddenly a pair of cold hands picked her up by the neck and banged her head several times against the mattress.

The woman experienced four such sessions of diabolical assault. After the second attack, the former JW states, "I dreamt that I was in a dark basement. At the top were little windows with sunlight shining through, and in the room were Jehovah's Witnesses from everywhere, all the ones I knew, including my brother-in-law. I was frantically trying to climb up the walls to get out of the basement. But everyone kept holding my legs. I was crying and screaming because I couldn't get out."

The third psychic attack occurred one afternoon when she was comparing what the *Watchtower* said concerning certain events in Revelation with what Armstrongism taught. (In her desperate search for spiritual truth, the poor woman was ready to jump from one false religion into another.)

Feeling tired, she lay down; no sooner had she done so

than a "presence" came through the window. A terrifying icy coldness gripped her body and held it in a state of paralysis. Then a voice spoke and said, "What are you going to do, Mary?" After asking this question, the entity from hell burst into a fit of demonic laughter. The woman was nearly out of her mind with fright. Seeking out the Evangelical church her deceased grandmother used to attend, she gave her heart to God when the altar call was given. Weeping her way through to God, she was gloriously saved and delivered.

Another woman writes that her married daughter became aware of being demon-possessed upon leaving the Jehovah's Witnesses. Ordinarily the young lady was a very modest girl, but one day an uncontrollable power made her take off all her clothes, cut off her hair, and go up and down the street, calling on neighbors! It seems that the devil wanted to humiliate her for leaving the JW organization.

The young lady says that "a vicious beast" controlled her actions all that day. She remembers everything that happened but was powerless to resist the "will" of the awful "thing" dominating her. Concerned Christians prayed for her, and that night she felt the evil power leave her body never to return. Today she is a fine Christian woman who attends an Evanglical church.

Generally speaking, cultists of every stripe are allowed a certain amount of free movement in this world. Like an inmate in a penitentiary, if a prisoner obeys the rules and does not attempt to escape, he is allowed to move around virtually unmolested. But just let him try to break out and see what happens. The prison guards with their vicious hounds will be hot on his trail.

It is a different matter, however, if the governor of the state grants some prisoner a parole. The prisoner is permitted to walk away a free man, and no one can molest him. If the concerned spiritual prisoner will beseech the Governor of the universe, the Lord Jesus Christ, he will be granted a full pardon, enabling him to freely leave the kingdom of darkness for the kingdom of God's dear Son.

The former spiritualist medium, Victor H. Ernest, relates the following incident that occurred in a seance he attended:

> When the trumpet returned for my third and last question, I reviewed what the spirit had said. 'O spirit, you believe that Jesus is the Son of God, that he is the Savior of the world . . . do you believe that Jesus died on the cross and shed his blood for the remission of sin?' The medium, deep in trance, was catapulted off his chair. He fell in the middle of the living room and lay groaning as if in deep pain. The turbulent sounds suggested spirits in a carnival of confusion.[2]

These examples clearly show how much the demonic spirits fear and hate the blood of Christ. The reason why evil spirits go into a paroxysm of rage and terror at the mention of Christ's blood will be discussed in the last chapter of this book.

[2] Victor H. Ernest, *I Talked with Spirits* (Wheaton, Ill.: Tyndale House, 1970), p. 32.

6.

Knowing the Future

■ Why are people so preoccupied with knowing the future? Natural man has an inquisitive nature; he wants to know what tomorrow, next week, and the following months have to offer, because, without God, his only security rests in whatever he can arrange for himself. Without God, he is ruled by anxiety, at best, about the future, if not outright fear. Or greed. Or lust for power. Or ambition, which is practically the same thing.

But ironically, knowing the future would mean that all the accumulated problems and sorrows of days and weeks yet to come would burst into your mind *now!* Many people can't cope with the problems of today, let alone all the grief and heartaches of days and weeks not yet spent. We would do well to heed our Lord's wise admonition concerning the future: "Take therefore no thought for the morrow: for the morrow shall take thought for the things of itself. Sufficient unto the day is the evil thereof" (Matt. 6:34).

Moreover, the Lord Jesus clearly stated,: "It is not for you to know the times or the seasons, which the Father hath put in his own power" (Acts 1:7). Man's audacious attempt to wrest secrets from the future is a direct violation of God's will. All divination—whether it be by crystal-ball gazing, fortune-telling, Ouija boards, spiritism, astrology, or necromancy—is an attempt to circumvent the divine will.

The following declaration is found in Holy Scripture: "Yet man is born unto trouble, as the sparks fly upward" (Job 5:7). It is the lot of imperfect man to suffer hardship, disappointment, sorrow, sickness, pain, anguish, and finally death. These negative influences plague mankind from the cradle to the grave; from youth to hoary age rolls the tide of human woe. Man eternally struggles to rise above these destructive forces; yet try as he may, man cannot overcome them, not by his own power, nor by the dark powers of occultism. The best he can do is to attempt to cope with the problems of life, avoid thinking about those that are beyond him, and escape reality, which is fraught with the utter lack of meaning in his life.

But Holy Scripture also teaches that God has a glorious destiny in store for mankind: man is to ultimately rise above the stars. His eternal home will be a land that is fairer than day, where saints immortal reign. The indescribable beauty of another world—a world without pain, suffering, sorrow or death—will be his to enjoy forever. But not all the sons of men will reach heaven's golden shore. Christ makes this fact very clear when He tells us, "Broad is the way, that leadeth to destruction, and many there be which go in thereat: Because strait is the gate, and narrow is the way, which leadeth unto life, and few there be that find it" (Matt. 7:13).

Why does God allow troubles to afflict mankind? Consider the precious stone called a diamond. It takes nature thousands of years to produce a diamond. Tremendous pressure and intense heat had to be applied to some worthless piece of carbon before it could become a precious sparkling diamond. The Scriptures teach that it is God's will for man to enjoy a

better existence than what he now has in this present evil
world. But in order to prepare man for that realm of immortal bliss, where endless fountains of pure joy abound, he must
needs be tried, proven, and made ready. His character must
be tested. Man must be put through the crucible of suffering
and the fires of affliction so that he might come forth as pure
gold. It is the hardships, trials, and reversals in life that really
make a person. Our sentiments here are best expressed in the
following words of Holy Scripture: "Wherein ye greatly rejoice, though now for a season, if need be, ye are in heaviness
through manifold temptations: That the *trial of your faith,*
being much more precious than of gold that perisheth,
though it be tried with fire, might be found unto praise and
honour and glory at the appearing of Jesus Christ" (I Pet.
1:6–7).

The strains and stresses of life are allowed to come upon us
so that we might cling closer to God. A Christian meets the
challenges of life head-on. He takes comfort in the precious
promises of God's Word. Certainly the Lord has given His
people many wonderful promises; here are but two of them:
"I will never leave thee, nor forsake thee" (Heb. 13:5). Again
we read, "Lo, I am with you alway, even unto the end of the
world" (Matt. 28:20). Life was never intended to be a bed of
roses. This world should be viewed primarily as a training
ground to prepare man's soul for the glories of eternity. How
we live in this world determines our eternal destiny.

People who are interested in the future would do well to
seriously study the Bible instead of dabbling with the occult.
Hundreds of prophecies are to be found in the Bible, and a
number of them have been literally fulfilled to the letter.
Prophecy is history written before it happens. Bible scholars
inform us that on the day of Christ's crucifixion more than
twenty different prophecies were fulfilled.

Within the pages of Holy Writ, the whole drama of humanity is unfolded—the life, death, and eternal destiny of man are clearly outlined. The wonderful promises found in God's blessed Word enable the dying Christian to pillow his head in peace. Holy Scripture assures the believing heart that there will be eternal comradeship with loved ones and friends of like precious faith in that fairer land beyond the sunset. To the Christian is promised a wonderful future, a future as boundless and great as the universe itself.

The soul of man cries out for truth, but it is only God's Book that can fully meet this great, pent-up need within the human breast. The Bible is the believer's compass and guide; it is his chart through the Sea of Life. Only the precepts found in God's Word can guide us safely through the treacherous waters of life. There is a beautiful haven of rest over on eternity's shore, yet only those who believe the Gospel of Jesus Christ will be allowed to enter.

The Bible is unquestionably the greatest book ever written. It is not only the most popular, but also the most hated, attacked, and vilified book of all time. Men who have believed its sacred pages have been burned alive, torn asunder, ravaged by wild beasts, imprisoned, beaten, driven from their homes, and made the off-scourings of the earth. God's Word has been subjected to bitterest criticism. God-haters have challenged and tested to the very limit every statement, clause, and precept found in the Bible. None of the hellish attacks ever launched against the Bible have ever been able to disprove one verse of Scripture. The old hymn writer summed it up well: "The Bible stands like a rock undaunted, towering o'er the wrecks of time."

The Bible has a majesty of utterance that no book of man has ever approached. Its beauty of expression and captivating truths have become immortal poetry. If only the weary in heart would believe the Bible's divine message of love and grace, they would find that peace of God which passeth all understanding.

The honest inquirer may wonder how we know the Bible is true. One of the many reasons is simply: it works. When a person sincerely believes with all his heart in God, and accepts the Bible as God's revelation to man, then acts on these facts, things *will* happen. Faith sets into motion the divine laws of God. It is written, "But without faith it is *impossible* to please him: for he that cometh to God must believe that he is, and that he is a rewarder of them that diligently seek him" (Heb. 1:6).

The Bible contains many promises, and some of them can be fulfilled here and now in every person's life, but the seeker must meet certain conditions. Here is one of the great assuring statements found in the pages of Holy Writ: "He that believeth on the Son of God *hath the witness in himself*" (I John 5:10).

Something wonderful and tremendous happens when a person truly believes in Christ. What happens is that God's Holy Spirit gives the believer a miraculous witness in his heart that Christ is indeed alive and real. Another text corroborating this same truth declares, "The Spirit itself beareth witness with our spirit, that we are the children of God" (Rom. 8:16). We thus see that God gives His believing children real assurance of acceptance when they truly belong to him.

The question is naturally raised, "How does such a thing work?" The following analogy may help us to better understand. We know it is impossible to explain the intricate process called assimilation. No one rally understands how the food we eat is converted into flesh, blood, sinew, bone, and strength. Here is one of the mysteries man has never been really able to solve. We may not know how to intellectually explain the process of assimilation, yet within our bodies there has been imparted an intuitive knowledge enabling this very necessary function to take place. All we know intellectually is that food eaten gives the necessary strength and health to carry out our daily tasks. It would be utterly ludicrous for one not to eat food merely because he didn't *intellectually* understand the complex workings of assimilation.

The same can be said concerning God and the Bible. When we partake of spiritual food, our souls are being fed with that hidden manna from heaven. Each believer derives from God's Word the spiritual strength that, if appropriated, will enable him to become more than conqueror over the world, the flesh, and the devil. When one is genuinely "born again," he is keenly aware that everything in Holy Scripture is true, because God has planted into his very soul "intuitive wisdom" concerning spiritual things.

7.

Spiritualism

■ Instead of accepting what the Bible teaches about eternity, spiritualists have given themselves over to seek after "spirits" in order to learn what happens after death.

The basic belief of spiritualism has to do with the continuation of life after death. What we call existence after death in itself is certainly not wrong, for such is the plain teaching of the Bible. Spiritualists, however, go beyond the permitted boundaries of the biblical doctrine of immortality and attempt to set up, contrary to divine will, communication between the living and the dead. This kind of rapport is usually established through the agency of a psychic or medium who willingly permits supernatural entities to possess and speak through him. The possibility of humans establishing contact with spirits from beyond is the central teaching in spiritualism.

Spiritualism has been called the cult of antiquity. Away back in the Book of Exodus, we learn that the ancient Egyptians practiced necromacy (consulting the dead) and other occult arts. The sorcerers at Pharaoh's court had such occult power that they could even duplicate several of the miracles

Moses had performed. Biblical and secular history both testify to the fact that the ancient Egyptians, Babylonians, Chaldeans, and Canaanites all practiced various forms of spiritism. Holy Scripture strongly warns us that God's curse is upon all those who indulge in spiritism or any other occult practice.

While interviewing a medium one day, I asked, "What was it that made you turn to spiritualism?" He replied that the great questions pertaining to eternity had aroused his interest, and spiritualism had given him actual proof that there is indeed a spirit world. Because of his obsession with psychic matters, the spirits have endowed this man with a certain healing power. Also he has been allotted a special spirit guide—a spirit monk! This medium holds seances in his home regularly, and I have been told that a number of people have been healed at his meetings.

During my interview with him, which lasted nearly four hours, I also had an opportunity to speak with the medium's wife. She is also a medium, one who demonstrates the art of psychometry, the power to "read" either a living or a dead person by handling some article which belonged to the person. Some psychometric clairvoyants claim to have the ability, not only to tell the past, but also the future of a person by interpreting the psychic impressions received from any article that belongs to the person. Certain clairvoyants who have this gift are able to take a sick person's handkerchief, even though the ill person is not present, and name the actual disease afflicting him.

I do not know to what extent the woman I was talking with has developed her gift, except that she teaches psychometry at a psychic school. The spiritualist couple were pleasant and charming. They have a little girl about four years old, and I was told that she has "a spirit playmate." Both parents have watched their little girl play and carry on conversations with an unseen spirit entity.

I was further told that their daughter has had several nocturnal visitors. On one occasion, the mother heard her child talking to someone in the dead of night. The mother got out of bed went to the child's room and asked, "Honey, who were you talking to?" The daughter replied, "Just a nice lady who comes and visits me after I'm in bed." Some days later, the child happened to be playing with her mother's purse, when a photo fell out of it and landed on the floor. Upon seeing it, she cried out, "Mommy, here's a picture of the lady who visits me after I go to bed!" The mother was stunned; the picture that had fallen out of her purse was of the childs grandmother, who had died before the child was born.

SPIRITUALISM AND HEALING

Another time this same child got very sick, and her parents took her to the doctor. Seemingly, the medical treatment prescribed did not help. The parents became quite concerned and decided to hold a special spiritualist healing service for their little girl. That night the child cried out in bed, and the mother rushed to her. She said she was scared because a man had stood by her bed and laid his hands on her. Next morning the child was perfectly well and has not been sick since.

Incidents of this kind have thoroughly convinced the spiritualist parents that they are in contact with good spirits. Such happenings do frequently occur in spiritualist circles. Does the Christian church have an answer to the "good works" performed by spirits?

It is well to remember that Satan does not always appear with the face of evil. He most certainly can perform good deeds, if it's in his interest to do so. How weighty is the caution of Saint Paul when he says, "And no marvel; for Satan himself is transformed into an angel of light" (II Cor. 11:14).

How cunning and deceptive are the ways of this dark prince of subterfuge. An angel of light would naturally perform good works, and it is a relatively easy thing for Satan and his demon messengers to pose as good spirits, and even meet the needs of people, if it suits their purpose. A strong warning must be issued at this juncture: every time the devil does a favor for someone, there is a "pay-back"—often excruciatingly exacted.

Those who are knowledgeable regarding occult matters know that in black magic there are not only rites for revenge and persecution, but also spells and enchantments for healing. Even the witch doctors in heathen countries can accomplish healings through evil spirits. All disease and sickness emanates from Satan. If it will promote his overall plan of deception or bring people under his dominion, the devil can remove his paw from one who is a victim of sickness.

This is precisely what happens in spiritualist healing meetings. We do not deny that people are healed in spiritualism. However, the only supernatural healing *coming from God today* is done in the name of our Lord Jesus Christ. You will recall that our Savior made the following announcement just before He went back to heaven: "And these signs shall follow them that believe; In my name shall they cast out devils; they shall speak with new tongues; They shall take up serpents; and if they drink any deadly thing, it shall not hurt them; they shall lay hands on the sick, and they shall recover" (Mark 16:17–18).

Please note that *God's power* to heal the sick and to cast out devils can flow only when the name of Christ is invoked. Since spiritualists cannot tap God's power, their wonders and miracles of healing must come from the only other source of supernatural power, from him who is the "ape of God," Satan the devil.

A businessman wrote Harry Edwards, famous spiritualist leader in England, seeking his help to get rid of a cyst on his wrist. He received a letter from Mr. Edwards stating that his healing would begin shortly. One week later, the cyst vanished! During the following months, this man began reading Christian books put out by former mediums exposing occultism. Eventually he came to the conclusion that the help he had received came from a demonic source. Shaken by such a revelation of truth, he renounced Harry Edwards, and every contact with demonic spirits. In one week, the cyst returned! He writes, "This should be proof to anyone dabbling in this area that the spirits who did the healing were not of God, but rather were evil spirits who took revenge when I renounced them."

SPIRITUALISM AND THE BIBLE

It is important for us to remember that spiritualists reject not only Christ's divinity but also our Lord's resurrection from the dead. Many who have embraced this false system do not even believe in a personal God or a personal devil. It is quite true that spiritualists often use the term "God," but they have re-defined the term to suit their own purpose. When a spiritualist speaks of "God," he is really referring to "infinite intelligence," and to them, this merely means a "supreme *im*personal power."

The Bible doctrine of hell is also denied by those who follow the dark pathway of spiritualism. Voices, apparently speaking from beyond the veil in spiritualist meetings, would have us believe that "the doorway to reformation is never closed in the spirit world." This is a lie! God's Word plainly declares, "How shall we escape, if we neglect so great salvation?" (Heb. 2:3). Holy Writ clearly states that there is no hope for those who die unprepared to meet God. People must make their peace with God here and now; those who put off doing so will incur eternal anguish and everlasting tribulation. If men disregard the many opportunities God gives them to repent and get right with Him, then, the Bible declares, "There remaineth no more sacrifice for sins, But a certain fearful looking for of judgment and fiery indignation, which shall devour the adversaries" (Heb. 10:26–27).

We might add that the biblical doctrine of Christ's vicarious atonement is flatly rejected by spiritualists. The great Bible truth that only Christ's precious shed blood can atone for man's sin is hated by every spiritualist. They prefer to accept the messages of their so-called spirit guides who tell them that man reaches perfection through progressive evolution in the spirit world.

That some dark sinister hand has indeed injected the disciples of spiritualism with a venomous hatred for the blood of Christ was brought forcefully home to me some years ago when I was challenged by a group of spiritualists.

Early one summer evening I was engaged in street witnessing and handing out tracts. While I was doing so, three people passed me, and I offered them one of my pamphlets dealing with judgment and hell. Scanning it, one of the women sharply rebuked me for handing out such "rubbish" to people on the street. In the course of our conversation it came out that these people were spiritualists, on their way to a meeting. Upon discovering this fact, I asked them, "Do you people believe in demons?" The medium glared at me and sarcastically replied that I should come with them and see for myself.

The tone in which these words were spoken left me with the distinct impression that I was being challenged. Going back to my car, I prayed about the matter and asked God for protection and guidance. Feeling that God wanted me to witness to these people, I ventured for the first time through the doors of a spiritualist meeting place.

From the moment I took my seat in that Spiritualist church, I continued to pray and ask God to grant me an opportunity to bear a good witness for Him. The spiritualists began their meeting that night by singing a few hymns. Leafing through the spiritualist hymnal, I noticed that the name of Christ was absent.

The woman minister gave a short discourse attacking the Christian teaching of judgment to come and hell. She then proceeded to walk up and down the aisles prophesying over people. The meeting concluded, and it was time to disperse and go home.

After the service was dismissed, an opportunity presented itself for me to speak with the medium. In the course of our conversation, I asked, "Why is it your hymnal doesn't have any songs of praise for the Lord Jesus Christ? Why are there no songs concerning the birth of Christ? Neither is there any mention of Christ's death or of His resurrection from the dead!"

My last question really stirred things up in that place: "Why do you people not have any songs in your hymnbook that speak about the blood of Jesus Christ? Don't you know that it is only Christ's precious shed blood that can take away man's sin? Have you never read, 'It is the blood that maketh an atonement for the soul'? (Lev. 17:11). 'And the blood shall be to you for a token upon the houses where ye are, *and when I see the blood I will pass over you*'? (Exod. 12:13). 'And without the shedding of blood is no remission'? (Heb. 9:22).

"God's Holy Book further tells us that man is redeemed, not with corruptible things such as silver and gold, 'but with the precious blood of Christ, as of a lamb without blemish and without spot' (I Pet. 1:19)."

The next Scripture made a spiritual explosion: "Do you not know that it is written, *'The blood of Jesus Christ His Son cleanseth us from all sin'*? (1 John 1:7)."

While I was in the midst of quoting this text, suddenly the medium to whom I was speaking went into a trance. The flesh on her neck started to twitch violently and move involuntarily. Stranger still was the manifestation of stammering lips that had now come upon her.

Seeing what was happening caused something to stir within me. In a firm, commanding voice, I heard myself say to the medium, "The devil hates the blood of Christ, does he not?" In response to my inquiry, the entranced medium loudly shouted, "Yes! Yes! Yes!" I then heard myself say to the medium's spirit control, "You also are one who hates the blood of Christ!"

Immediately that voice speaking through the medium replied with a distinct hissing "Yessss."

Meanwhile the other spiritualists had formed a circle around me. When the medium acknowledged that Satan does indeed hate the blood of Christ, several persons in the circle went into a demonic fit and began emitting weird guttural sounds and animal-like cries.

I pleaded with all in that place to renounce spiritualism, and accept Christ as Lord and Savior. But no one replied. Not a word was spoken. And despairing for their souls, I left.

Suddenly, a man came charging out the door and ran after

me across the street. When he reached me, he stopped and shouted, "God bless you! God bless you! God bless you!"

But I felt only revulsion in my spirit. Putting out my hand toward him, I said, "Let me pray for you." His eyes widened, and he ran back into the hall.

For a long time I puzzled over what this spiritualist really meant when he shouted the blessing of his spiritualist god at me. It was only after I had made a thorough study of witchcraft, particularly the practice of black magic, that the full import of this incident dawned on me.

It is the Christian view that the god of all occult practitioners, including spiritualists, is none other than the dark prince of this world, Satan. The following incident that took place at a spiritualist meeting will help verify this fact: "At a seance, the controlling spirit, through the medium, Mrs. Connant, was asked 'Do you know of any person we call the devil?' 'We certainly do,' was the reply, 'And yet this same devil is our God, our Father!' " [1]

When the spiritualist man had shouted the blessing of his god upon me, he was actually uttering a curse. Everything in witchcraft is reversed. Good is branded as evil, and evil is called good! In black magic ceremonies, the Christian cross is turned upside down as a symbol of contempt and utter rejection of Christianity. I have seen more than a few hippies walking down the street, wearing large inverted crosses around their necks. This is their "thing," and they do it to flaunt their hatred of Christ and to show the world they are servants of Satan. Likewise, in witchcraft ceremonies, the Bible is turned upside down, and the Lord's prayer read backward. These things are done in order to please the demons so they will be more disposed to grant favors.

[1] *Banner of Light*, November 4, 1865.

Thus we see that, in actual fact, Satan's blessing is a curse. Consequently, when the spiritualist had invoked his god to bless me, the spirits controlling this poor man got him to pull what is called in occultism "a psychic trigger." This act can only be performed by a human will, and once it is done, the demonic forces are mobilized and then unleashed against the intended victim. The full force of Satan's fury is then hurled forth from the dark abyss, and payment must be made for use of it.

If perchance, the would-be victim is protected by some higher power, or is in league with a demon of greater rank than that of his assailant, then the curse boomerangs and comes back on him who released "the psychic trigger." Black magicians are well aware of the inherent dangers in "the conjuration of destruction." It is reported that a number of occultists have lost their sanity and even their lives by indulging in this dangerous practice.

AUTOMATIC WRITING

Many varied ways are used by spiritualist mediums to contact spirits. One method that is employed is called automatic writing. How does it work? The "sensitive" takes a pencil and holds it lightly over some writing paper. Putting her mind and body into a relaxed and passive state, the sensitive then waits for a surge of supernatural power to come upon her writing hand. If the medium is adept, she will not have to wait many minutes before some strange power begins to move her pen. Some have reported that the pen moved so fast they could hardly hold on to it! After the "spirit control" has given his written message, the power controlling the medium's hand lifts, and she reverts back to a normal state.

There on the writing paper is an elaborate composition, often written *in another handwriting*.

It should be noted that in many cases the person doing automatic writing goes into a trance and is semi-conscious; others go into various other stages between full consciousness and complete unconsciousness during their period of automatic writing. Foreign languages, unknown to the automatist, have been fluently written by the medium under this power, and a good deal of poetry, art, and music have, likewise, been automatically produced. Such esteemed men of letters as Victor Hugo, Goethe, Victorien Sardow, and others have produced automatic writings.

Another form of automatic writing employs a "planchette." This instrument was devised by a well-known French spiritualist, M. Planchette, in 1853, for the express purpose of communicating with spirits. Some fifteen years later, a toy-making firm in America got hold of the planchette and started flooding the country with them. The mechanism is made of a thin heart-shaped piece of wood which rests on two small wheel-casters with a pen pointing downward acting as a third support. The one using it places his hand on the wood, and the pencil writes automatically. Some mediums claim that through the planchette their spirit-control has given them manuscripts that are now published works.

People who indulge in automatic writing have been known to develop very serious psychic disturbances in their life. The noted German parapsychologist Rudolf Tischer tells us that when one yields to every wish and urge to indulge in automatic writing, it can get such a hold that one is no longer in control of one's own body, but ends up a slave who must obey the every whim of the demonic fiend that now possesses him. If he refuses to go along with the commands and suggestions of the controlling spirit entity, very unpleasant, even horrid things will happen to him.

Tischer tells us that he knew a woman who did a lot of automatic writing. One day he was with her and her husband in a coffee shop. While all three of them were having lunch, an overwhelming urge came upon the woman to do automatic writing. Her husband violently objected and said, "No, no, not here!" Some unseen force broke the woman's perspiring resistance, seized her hand, and began to bang and thump it angrily on the marble table. So much noise was being made by her hand slamming on the table that it drew the attention of other patrons. Tischer says the incident was so embarrassing he and his two guests fled from the restaurant in haste.[2]

One woman was driven to the brink of insanity and suicide through automatic writing. Her first contact with occult power was when she attended a spiritualist meeting. Upon arriving home after the service she heard a "voice" telling her to take up pencil and paper and to begin writing. When the woman obeyed, a strange power took control of her hand and began to draw a ship floundering in the midst of angry waves. When she had completed the spirit drawing, the "voice" then told her to lie down, which she did. From that moment on, she was completely taken over and controlled by demons.

The outside "voice" that first *asked* her to do things was now on the inside *giving orders*. One of the commands given her was that she abstain from all food for two weeks. So fully was the woman possessed by demons that they dictated her every movement. They even told her that she was chosen to bear the Christ child. On another occasion, the chief demon ordered her to take poison. Just as she was ready to obey and

2 *Ergebnisse Okkulter Forschung* p. 42–43.

swallow the deadly concoction, an unseen force knocked the glass out of her hand. Finally the poor woman ended up in a psychiatric ward at Vancouver General Hospital. Strange as it may seem, the demons stopped tormenting their victim during her stay in hospital. (They wanted her out of there.) Upon her release from the hospital, the demons resumed their cruel harassment once again. It was only after deep prayer that the woman was delivered. Today she is a victorious Christian who is a living witness to the delivering power of our Lord Jesus Christ.

Dr. Wickland writes about a lady of refinement who had artistic tastes. This person started practicing automatic writing and soon developed a harsh violent personality. Rubbing her temples, this woman would cry out at the top of her voice, "God save me! God save me!" Often she would run out into the street and throw herself in the mud—screaming, praying, and refusing to eat—declaring that if she dared to eat before six o'clock, demons would take her to hell.

D. D. HOME AND "TRIAL BY FIRE"

One of the most remarkable mediums in all the annals of spiritualism was Daniel Dunglas Home. He was converted to spiritualism in the year 1850 at the age of seventeen. Home's mediumship abilities were reported to have been outstanding. The following is an eyewitness account of one who beheld some of Home's more astonishing occult feats of magic:

Home got up and walked about the room. He was both elongated and raised in the air. . . . He then said to us, 'Do not be afraid and on no account leave your places.' We heard Home go into the next room, heard the window thrown up, and presently Home appeared standing upright outside our window. (The third

floor). He opened the window and walked in quite coolly. . . .
He then sat down laughing.[3]

This incredible happening was witnessed not only by Lord
Adare, correspondent for the *London Daily Telegraph* in Ab-
yssinia in 1867 and who later became Under-Secretary of
State for the Colonies, but it was also witnessed by the Earl
of Crawford, a Fellow of the Royal Society. Lord Adare's
cousin, Captain Wynn, was the third witness.

Another brilliant man who intensely investigated the great
physical medium D. D. Home was Sir William Crookes, dis-
coverer of thallium and monium. For his contributions to science, he was knighted and received the Order of Merit. It
was the report of this scientist that he could find no "natural"
explanation for the uncanny magical abilities of D. D. Home,
medium extraordinary. Sir William Crookes stated in the
Quarterly Journal of Science, January, 1871, that "there are at
least a hundred recorded instances of Mr. Home's rising
from the ground."

Home's ability to handle red-hot coals was repeated on a
number of occasions. Lord Lindsay tells us that Home had
placed red hot coals in his, Lindsay's, hands on eight occasions. Not once was there ever any injury. He further adds,
"A few weeks ago, I was at a seance with eight others. Of
these, seven held a red-hot coal without pain, and two others
could not bear the approach of it; of the seven, four were la-
dies." [4]

In his book, *Experiences in Spiritualism*, Lord Adare
writes:

[Home] went back to the fire, and with his hands stirred the em-
bers into a flame; then kneeling down, he placed his face right

[3] Lord Adare, *Experiences in Spiritualism with D. D. Home.*
[4] Report of the Dialectical Society's Committee on Spiritualism.

among the burning coals, moving it about as though bathing it in water. Then getting up, he held his finger for some time in the flame of the candle. Presently he took the same lump of coal he had previously handled and came over to us, blowing upon it to make it brighter. He then walked slowly around the table, and said, "I want to see which of you will be the best subject. Ah! Adare will be easiest because he has been most with Dan" (i.e., himself). Mr. Jencken held out his hand, saying, "Put it in mine." Home said, "No, touch it and see." He touched it with the tip of his finger and burnt himself. Home then held it within four or five inches of Mr. Sarl's and Mr. Hart's hands, and they could not endure the heat. He came to me and said, "Now, if you are not afraid, hold out your hand." I did so, and having made two rapid passes over my hand, he placed the coal in it. I must have held it for half a minute, long enough to have burned my hand fearfully; the coal felt scarcely warm. Home then took it away, laughed and seemed much pleased.

The ordeal by fire is still practiced today in heathen countries. It was a well-known custom among the Hindu people that those suspected of committing crimes could prove their innocence only by walking barefoot over red-hot coals. If they could do this and remain unhurt, it meant the gods had intervened to establish their innocence. Surprisingly, many who were forced to take the fire test came through it without injury. But others were badly burned and suffered terribly. We are told this cruel method remained in use up until the last century, when it was finally stamped out.

It is known that the priestesses of a Cappodocian goddess, Diana Parasya, were able to walk barefooted on red-hot coals without the least injury to themselves. Their invulnerability to fire was attributed to the powers of a divinity they worshiped.

In medieval Europe there existed what was called the trial by fire. The suspected criminal was often forced to undergo the ordeal of hot iron. This cruel pagan rite consisted of the suspect picking up and carrying red-hot irons in his bare hands, or walking barefoot over glowing iron bars, or thrusting his hand into a glowing iron gauntlet! The suspect was usually given a choice of one of these three ways in which to prove his innocence.

In our present day, we still have people who walk through fire in order to prove that their heathen gods have power to protect them. The pagan rite is practiced in India, Fiji, South Africa, Japan, New Zealand, and more recently in the hills of California.

One of the most amazing present-day accounts of fire-walking appeared in the *Pisgah Christian Paper* of March 1971. The story concerns a missionary from South Africa, the Reverend J. L. de Bruin, who was visiting the United States. He had gone with other spectators to watch Hindu sorcerers at their annual fire-walking ceremony.

Midway through the heathen ceremony, de Bruin was recognized by certain sorcerers who boasted that their gods had greater power than Christ. He was taunted, jeered, and personally challenged by the fire-walkers to try to duplicate what they could do through the power of their mighty gods. Praying in his heart how to answer them, the man of God suddenly felt a divine calmness come over his body and soul. He accepted their challenge and walked not once, but three times through a bed of fire thirty-three feet long, ten feet wide, and ten inches deep, full of red-hot burning coals. Ordinarily a Christian never attempts to perform wonders of this kind. However, like Elijah of old, he accepted their challenge to prove that God could protect him. And he has a motion-picture film, taken by a tourist, showing him walking barefooted through the bed of fire. Is it not written, "And when thou walkest through the fire, thou shalt not be burned. Neither shall the flame kindle upon thee"? (Isa. 43:2).

8.

Divination

■ As we have seen in the preceding chapters, ever since the dawn of human history, inquisitive man has tried to pierce the veil which separates the present from the future. Divination is one attempt to obtain illegitimate knowledge of the unknown. The ways of practicing this ancient mystical art are numerous and varied. All are strictly forbidden by God's word:

> There shall not be found among you any one that maketh his son or his daughter to pass through the fire, or that useth divination, or an observer of times, or an enchanter, or a witch. (Deut. 18:10)

Occultism offers the temptation of "forbidden wisdom." You will recall that Satan used this very approach to deceive Eve. Displaying serpent-like subtlety, the devil promised mother Eve that her eyes would be opened, and she would become wise as the gods. All she had to do was partake of the forbidden fruit. The same temptation is to be found in occultism. Partake of that which God forbids, *and wisdom will be yours!* But, oh, the price one must pay for a few nuggets of fool's gold!

Claims of the occult masters and their fraternities are grand beyond words. Using extravagant word coloring, they promise to take you through the gateway into unseen realms. The credulous are told that the Infinite is within their grasp. All they have to do is open up their psychic centers and contact "the Great Superbeings of the universe."

Unsuspecting people are led to believe they can expand their consciousness of the universe, and even become godlike by establishing individual mastership of the spheres. Those who take such esoteric teachings seriously are promised a personal vital role in the cosmic order of things.

Who among us doesn't want to have his eyes opened? Who wouldn't like to be more wise? Who wouldn't want to know the wisdom of the ages? Yet the Bible clearly states, "This wisdom descendeth not from above, but is earthly, sensual, *devilish*" (James 3:15). Secret knowledge is the bait used by occultists to lead unwary souls into Satan's web of deception and to feed the egos of those who think they are entering with their eyes open. Well, Satan's occult packages may be wrapped in fine tinsel and tied with attractive ribbon, but each package has within it a vile serpent from the Pit that will sting your soul to death.

ORACLES

The most popular form of divination practiced by the early Greeks was that of the Delphic Oracle. This was an ancient temple site built over a volcanic fissure where intoxicating vapors were said to issue forth from a cleft in the rocks. People from every station in Greek life came here annually for prophetic advice and magical help. The Arnold Prize Essay for 1859 gives the following graphic description of a Delphian priestess going into a trance state:

For one moment (the enquirer) saw a steaming chasm, a shaking tripod, above all, a Figure with fever on her cheek and foam upon her lips, who, fixing a wild eye upon space, tossed her arms aloft in the agony of her soul, and, with a shriek that never left his ears for days, chanted high and quick the dark utterances of the will of Heaven.

Another famous Greek oracle was the Oracle of Trophonius. A person who went to this place had to spend a night in the temple. While sleeping there, he would have wild, terrifying prophetic dreams which were interpreted next morning by the attending priests. Many other countries also had their shrines and oracles where a god, or demon, spoke to human beings through possessed priests and priestesses. The nations of antiquity all had their oracles where people could come and have consultations with demons.

The Assyrians practiced divination and other magical arts, and the Romans, in all likelihood, received their knowledge of occult matters from them. There is a striking similarity between the magical customs of both peoples, especially in regard to the consultation of oracles.

In *Collier's* magazine of October 26, 1946, Freling Foster writes regarding certain mediums in India who could get spirit entities to take over their bodies and speak through them while they were in a trance state. People would come from many miles around to get messages from the other side and to learn future events. The ollowing is his description of what takes place:

One of the queerest professions today is that of the Sungmas, the oracles of the Lamaist Church of Tibet. Each man professes to be the living abode of a particular spirit that, when he calls upon it, uses him as its medium to foretell future events or to bestow blessings. As proof that the spirit has taken over the control of his body, the Sungma passes into a trance and sways, jerks, dances, groans and foams at the mouth for half an hour. Every few minutes, however, he interrupts his maniacal antics to answer questions and allow worshippers to touch him, which is the purpose of his performance the price of which is based on the importance of the spirit.

ANTINOPOMANCY

One particularly loathsome form of divination practiced by ancient Egyptian sorcerers was antinopomancy, divining the future by consulting *the entrails of sacrificed children*. The Greek historian Herodotus relates that Menelaus, husband of the fair Helen of Troy, was hindered from leaving Egypt because the winds were contrary. While waiting for weather conditions to improve, Menelaus decided to satisfy his base curiosity by sacrificing two children so that his future destiny could be divined from their entrails. It is also recorded that Julian the Apostate, during his sorcery operations, had many children killed, solely for the purpose of consulting their entrails. The dark record of this infamous Roman emperor is full of evil and terrible reports. It was said that in Mesopotamia, Julian would lock himself in the Temple of the Moon and there practice every imaginable foul evil. After his death in battle, those who entered the Moon Temple were shocked to find a young woman hanging by her hair, with her liver ripped out! The Aztecs of Mexico worshiped their pagan demon deities in much the same manner. One of their cruel rites was to tear the hearts from the breasts of living persons in order to appease the demon gods they worshiped.

The pages of history tell us about a number of sorcerers who used the palpitating entrails of children in their foul magical rites. One black magic practitioner by the name of

Gilles de Rais and appointed marshal of France by Charles VII, was found guilty of this outrage in a court of law and executed on October 26, 1440.

Born in 1404, he fell heir to great riches and vast estates in Brittany. During his childhood, de Rais was brought up as a prince. It is said that as a youth he spent much time reading about the depravities of the Caesars from his large library of Latin manuscripts. The enormity of this man's crimes are shocking beyond description.

Servants of de Rais testified at his trial that they had seen him sacrifice children to Satan! One witness after the other told how de Rais took pleasure in the tortured death screams of his poor innocent victims.

Day after day the trial continued with horror being piled upon horror. The evidence was so overwhelming that de Rais finally broke down and confessed. Detail after gruesome detail was wrung out of him and brought to the light of day. When the evidence was all in, it was clearly proven that this monster had sacrificed over one hundred children to Satan.

Another writer states that at his trial, Gilles de Rais

> related how he had stolen away children, detailed all his foul cajolements, his hellish excitations, his frenzied murders, his ruthless rapes and ravishments; obsessed by the morbid vision of his poor pitiful victims, he described at length their long-drawn agonies or swift torturings; their piteous cries and the death-rattle in their throats; he avowed that he had wallowed in their warm entrails; he confessed that he had torn out their hearts through large gaping wounds, as a man might pluck ripe fruit.[1]

Diodorus Siculus, the Greek historian, mentions that the

[1] Montague Summers, *History of Witchcraft* (New York, N.Y.: University Books, 1956).

ancient Druids also practiced the abominable art of human sacrifice. He says:

> When they (the Druids) attempt divination upon important matters they practise a strange and incredible custom, for they kill a man by a knife-stab in the region above the midriff and after his fall they foretell the future by the convulsions of his limbs and the pouring of his blood, a form of divination in which they have full confidence, as it is of old tradition.[2]

Ghastly indeed was the method used by Druids to divine future happenings from a human sacrifice. The Roman historian Tacitus reports that the Druids, "consult the gods in the palpitating entrails of men," [3] while Strabo, the Greek geographer, relates that they would ritually stab their poor human victim in the back and then draw omens from his convulsive death agonies.[4]

Despicable practices such as antinopomancy are carried out by those who have totally abandoned themselves to evil. Certain demonic manuals state that the sacrifice of life (preferably human life) creates a propitious atmosphere for unholy magical ceremonies. It is said that demons are more favorably disposed to render aid when a sacrifice has been made to them. Scripture records an instance in which an animal has been sacrificed for the purpose of divination:

> For the king of Babylon stood at the parting of the way, at the head of the two ways, to use divination; he made his arrows bright, he consulted with images, he looked in the liver. (Ezek. 21:21)

[2] Diodorus Siculus, *Histories* V, 31, 2–5.
[3] Tacitus, *Annals*, XIV, 30.
[4] Strabo, *Geographica*, IV, 4.

BELOMANCY

Commenting upon the same passage in regard to divination by arrows, Saint Jerome states, "He shall stand in the highway, and consult the oracle after the manner of his nation, that he may cast arrows into a quiver, and mix them together, being written upon or marked with the names of each people, that he may see whose arrow will come forth, and which city he ought first to attack."

Belomancy, or divination by arrows, dates back to the Chaldeans and was also practiced by the Greeks and Arabs. The Arabs consecrated their divining arrows before the altar of some temple deity. They would then be carefully kept in the temple until needed.

Their divining arrows, consulted in times of major undertakings, were generally three in number. Upon one arrow would be the inscription, "My Lord doth forbid me"; the second would read, "My Lord doth command me"; and the third arrow would bear no inscription.

HYDROMANCY

Another form of divination called hydromancy (divining by water) dates back to ancient times. The seer would gaze at his own reflection in some rocky pool of water until a picture would appear showing him what he desired to know. It takes a lot of training and perseverance to successfully accomplish such an occult feat. The sensitive has to gaze down into either a pool or basin of water; during this procedure, he must become passive and let his mind go blank. In his subconscious mind, there has to be a yearning that some image other than his own will appear in the water.

Similar forms of divination are still practiced today in

Egypt where a boy splashes some ink into the palm of his hand; he will then gaze intently at the ink until pictures form that will answer those questions put to him by inquirers.

John Dee and Mirror Divination

In many parts of our world, peasant maidens consult their mirrors when the moon is full so that they might glimpse the features of their future husbands. Mirror-gazing is often used by occultists to induce a trance state. Cabalists, Rosicrucians, and other magic practitioners consider mirror-gazing to be a good way of tuning in to the astral plane. Mirrors are also used by black magicians to invoke demons. The following is a classic example, not just of mirror divination, but of what can happen when one dabbles in the occult.

John Dee was considered a genius in his day. He was of wealthy parentage and in 1548 at the age of only twenty-one was elected a fellow of Trinity College, Cambridge. Professor Dee was a brilliant mathematician, skillful lawyer, astronomer, and a trusted counselor to Queen Elizabeth. The reputation of his academic genius spread far and wide throughout all Europe. Many monarchs of that day offered Dee vast sums of money if he would consent to join their court. This much sought-after, brilliant young man had everything going for him; yet mirror divination led to his downfall.

Traveling throughout Europe, John Dee made it a point to meet the greatest wizards of his day. From his association with them, he developed an obsessive interest in occultism and spent much time studying the forbidden dark arts. Upon his return from England, Dee carried something back which he prized above the favor of kings and monarchs—a strange glass disc used for the purpose of divination!

Although surrounded with great wealth, luxury, and honors from the Queen, John Dee began living like a hermit, doing nothing else but studying the dark secrets of magic and sorcery. In his quest for knowledge of the unknown, he prayed day and night that divine wisdom might be granted him so that he might understand the great hidden mysteries of the universe.

So intent was Dee on realizing his perverse ambition that he stopped praying to God and started seeking help from Satan. His studies of occultism had taught him that when one seeks demonic aid, he forfeits his soul to Satan, but Dee's obsession was so powerful that no price seemed too great if the hidden wisdom of the ages could be his.

In fear and trembling he gathered together the necessary material to conjure up the devil. With mounting horror, Dee reached that point of climax in the dreadful Satanic ritual. Trembling, he peered into the glass disc. Beneath the cloudy surface of the glass, a hazy mist was swirling and moving as though agitated by some unseen hand, and suddenly a face without ears appeared in the glass. It was the face of a demon in the disguise of one Edward Kelley—sorcerer, rogue, murderer, who a year before had his ears hacked off in Lancaster for forgery.

This was the man Satan had chosen to be Dee's assistant. Persuaded that Kelley was the only one who could help him, Dee invited the Evil One's helper to join forces with him at his luxurious mansion. Both men now began to probe the polished glass disc in an attempt to learn hidden mysteries.

As the two wizards consulted the crystal disc, spirits appeared, giving them precise instructions. They are ordered to perform the most filthy rituals imaginable, even the smallest details of which had to be faithfully carried out or terrible punishment would befall them. They were forced to commit ritual murder, blackmail friends, and indulge in shameful sex practices. Spirits in the glass also ordered them to fill Mortlake mansion with expensive harlots; besides fulfilling their normal function, these fallen women were to be used in black magic ceremonies where ritual murders and tortures would be carried out.

Professor Dee had now been drawn into the very depths of occultism and could not get out. He was a helpless victim of the cruel devil that had been summoned from the abyss. It was impossible for him to back out. To do so would mean exposure, disgrace, ruin, death, and hell. Every day the two men had to appear at a given time before the polished glass disc to receive instructions. Yet Dee, in spite of his evil activities, still loved his young lovely wife dearly. While Dee and Kelley were consulting the mirror one day, the evil spirit gave them a new commandment. Both men were ordered to have their wives in common—or else! Dee was beside himself with anguish. He dared not go against the evil spirit's order. The doctor had sold his soul to the devil, and now it was time for the payback. This proved to be the crushing blow, for Dee's wife became so infatuated with Kelley that she would have nothing more to do with her husband.

Dee could take no more. He denounced Kelley to Emperor Rudolph as a worshiper of Satan, heretic, murderer, and a "son of the devil." Kelley was thrown into prison for his dastardly crimes. Some time later he attempted to escape, but the rope broke, and he fell to the ground, mortally injuring himself. Dying of his injuries, Kelley raved and roared about the devil in such a wild fearsome way that hardened prison hospital attendants, used to the most terrible deathbed scenes, refused to go near him.

Because of his involvement with Kelley and Satanism, John Dee was banished from Emperor Rudolph's court. All his wealth was confiscated, but he was permitted to keep the magic mirror. The common people in their rage had burned his luxurious mansion to the ground. Everything he had now lay in ruins. His priceless collection of rare magic manuscripts and books were all destroyed.

Dee lived on for another ten years. He who was considered one of the greatest minds of his age was broken in spirit and reduced to earning a living, so the record states, by reading horoscopes for the lower working classes and their wives.

The record tells us that he died alone, penniless, and when his remains were discovered, all he had was the worn-out clothes on his back, and wrapped in a bundle of rags, the magic mirror which he had been too terrified to use since his banishment from Emperor Rudolph's court. At the time of Dee's death, King James I was on the throne, and when he heard about Dee's magic mirror, he gave orders to destroy it. But by some quirk of fate, the mirror was not destroyed. We are told that in the eighteenth century, Dee's magic mirror was presented to the British Museum.[5]

A Modern Instance

When I was about sixteen, I was interested in weight lifting, and was working out at the YMCA one day, when I got acquainted with a young man whom I had never seen before. This chap—we'll call him Bill—had a well-developed physique and was exceptionally strong. I learned that he worked nights as a telegraph operator at a quiet train depot five miles out of town. Occasionally in the evenings I would go and visit him.

During one of my visits, he told me, "I want to develop my

[5] Lewis Spence, *An Encyclopedia of Occultism* (London: G. Routledge & Sons, 1920). Peter Robson, *The Devil's Own*.

psychic powers." He used to sit alone at night in a dark room before his mirror. On each side of the mirror would be a lighted candle, enabling him to dimly see his reflection in the glass. Hour after hour, Bill would gaze into the mirror; he would put his mind into a blank state so that vibrations from the realms beyond could be more easily received. His purpose: to make contact with the so-called ascended spiritual masters.

Bill's mirror-gazing did bring results—of a sort. The day-telegraph operator and his wife, who had an apartment over the office, started seeing weird apparitions in their bedroom at night. Bill told me that the frightened screams of the day-operator's wife were getting to him.

Bill was transferred to another area, and I never did see him again, but some months later a mutual friend told me that he had had a mental breakdown and had to be committed to an asylum.

THE OUIJA BOARD

A popular form of divination used today is the Ouija board. The manufacturer of this so-called toy, Parker Brothers of Salem, Massachusetts, is jubilant about its incredible sales. Since 1967, over twelve million Ouija boards have been sold in North America. This divining contraption outsells Monopoly!

When someone uses a Ouija board, he is, in actual fact, opening himself up to psychic influences. It is all the more dangerous because countless spirits are just waiting for people who want to contact occult powers. Even leading spiritualists have written warnings in our newspapers concerning the dangers one can encounter by using a Ouija board. Spiritualist mediums have told me of numbers of people who have become possessed by evil spirits through the Ouija board.

Case histories show that spirits of a particularly malevolent nature seem to delight in communicating with people through a Ouija board. Many spiritually ignorant parents buy Ouija boards at Christmas time for the children they love. According to one authority, Hans Holzer, "A child, a virgin, a sexual innocent is especially susceptible of being possessed. I know of a number of people who've been entered through the Ouija board, and let me tell you, it's a difficult and tedous task to rid an involuntary medium of a spirit."

Parents would be abhorred at the thought of their innocent child communicating with a sexual degenerate, but the entity that boys and girls communicate with through the Ouija board is far more wicked, perverted, and revolting than the worst child-molester stalking our streets today. Parents who permit their children to play with a Ouija board are unwittingly helping to create an unholy alliance between their own children and demons. Any parent who has a Ouija board in the house should take it out and burn it. Ray Jarman, in his book, *Pseudo-Christians*, reports one instance of a scream emanating from a burning Ouija board.

Innumerable cases are on record of people who have blown their minds through psychic experimentation, especially with automatic writing and the Ouija board. Carl A. Wickland, M.D., has this to say concerning Ouija boards:

The serious problem of alienation and mental derangement attending ignorant psychic experiments was first brought to my attention by the cases of several persons whose seemingly harmless experiences with automatic writing and the Ouija board resulted in such wild insanity that commitment to asylums was necessitated.[6]

Dr. Wickland in his book tells of several people who attempted suicide or went stark raving mad after experimenting with automatic writing and the Ouija board. He tells us of Mrs. E., who normally was "amiable, pious, quiet and refined, but became boisterous and noisy, romped about and danced, used vile language, and claiming she was an actress, insisted upon dressing for the stage. . . . Finally she became so irresponsible that she was placed in an asylum."

In Haney, British Columbia, a retired missionary tells a story about a group of teenagers in North Saskatchewan who, about six months earlier, had held a seance with a Ouija board. The board "told" them that within a year, six of them would be dead. Since that time, two had hanged themselves and one had drowned. The others, the man says, are terrified.

Some people have been shocked when they have asked the Ouija board the "source" of its information and it has truthfully answered, "the god of hell," "Satan," "the devil," or "hell."

OUIJA BOARDS AND DEMONS

One young lady the author interviewed had a harrowing experience after using the Ouija board. She had been reading books on witchcraft and other occult subjects for years. One afternoon she and two friends were using the Ouija board and the young lady asked the Ouija board if anything exciting was going to happen that day. "Yes," replied the Ouija board, "you will see the devil at six-thirty!"

Giggling, the three young women continued asking the

[6] Carl A. Wickland, *Thirty Years among the Dead* (London: Spiritualist P., 1968).

board various questions. Some questions were answered truthfully, and others were not. When five-thirty came, they decided to quit playing with the Ouija board, just in case the devil did decide to show up. Suddenly, a kind of paralysis came over them, and they were unable to move. In the open archway of a door leading into another room, a strange mist was beginning to form. The mist-like substance was then worked by some unseen master craftsman into a large black dog-like creature with bulging, red-glowing eyes, standing on its hind legs with bat wings outstretched and fierce-looking talons for paws. The three young women were now screaming with horror; two of them felt the hideous presence of evil when it first entered the room . . . yet they did not see the dreadful apparition! The only one who could see this thing from hell was the young woman being interviewed. This diabolical manifestation of evil slowly came across the room, touched the clairvoyant one on the neck, and disappeared. Immediately, Miss G's neck started to swell, and she became sick and was confined to bed for some time. When the power of evil lifted, Miss G's two girl friends fled from the house.

Lying in bed one night recuperating from her ordeal, Miss G saw the same demon go into her young sister's room. Horrified that the thing had come back, she was then astonished to see this hellish fiend flee from her sister's room. Wanting to know what it was that could chase a demon, she tiptoed into her sister's room. The sight she beheld melted her heart. There in the bed lay her young sister, full of innocence, and oh, such a look of peace, contentment, and serenity graced that child's face. One could not help but believe that guardian angels must be standing vigil over the child. And there on the night table near the little girl's bed was a copy of the Bible. The scene in her little sister's room that night had such a profound effect on Miss G that she gave her heart to Christ and is now saved and filled with God's Holy Spirit and attends a charismatic church.

NECROMANCY

Perhaps the most perilous form of divination is necromancy, consulting the dead! This particular occult art has been called "the touchstone of occultism," for if an adept can successfully accomplish this magical feat, he has proven his worth as a sorcerer.

There are three different types of necromancy. The most common form of this art is that of establishing rapport with the spirit of a dead person. We find that, for the most part, spiritualist mediums are involved with this aspect of necromancy. It should be remembered that mediums do not communicate with spirits of the dead; it is demons whom they contact, demons who impersonate the voices of the dead. And this is borne out by Holy Scripture, with one notable exception: the witch of Endor who summoned forth Samuel from the dead. In this particular case, God intervened to allow the real Samuel to appear and pronounce terrible judgment upon King Saul for seeking aid from a witch (I Sam. 28:7–19).

Another form of necromancy is the bringing forth of a visible manifestation of the dead. Genuine materialization mediums or witches are extremely rare; almost all who claim to be are fakes. To bring about a physical manifestation of the dead, tremendous amounts of energy have to be released from the medium's body in the form of ectoplasm, a thick vapor-like substance which oozes from the entranced medium's mouth, eyes, nose, ears, or stomach and is dimly visible in a dark room. Once the vaporous substance begins to flow forth, it gradually becomes solid upon hitting the air, and before the startled onlookers, this mass is sculptured by unseen hands into various shapes and forms. A spirit then takes possession of the ectoplasmic body and proceeds up and down the room ministering to those in attendance. I recall some years ago hearing the Reverend Bob McAlister, who has a missionary work in Brazil, speak on this subject. He told us that in Brazil there were some spiritualist mediums who had the power to perform this necromantic feat.

Former spiritualist Raphael Gasson tells us that he has witnessed this phenomenon a number of times. He mentions in his book, *The Challenging Counterfeit*, that photographs have been taken in the dark by a special camera showing weird sights of "ectoplasm hanging down like icicles from the mouth, nose, etc., of the medium." We are told that if the substance comes in contact with the light, or is touched without the permission of the controlling spirit, it recoils with a tremendous impact back into the medium's eyes, nose, mouth, or stomach before having a chance to dissolve back to its original state. Gasson relates that he has known mediums who have been blinded or crippled for life by the rebounding solid ectoplasm and has heard that this can cause death. In his own case, Gasson was blinded for twenty-four hours by the sudden springing back of the hardened substance. This is why, in most cases, demonstrations of mediumship are closed to the general public.

Another account dealing with the same phenomenon tells us that Sir William Crookes was given permission by the controlling spirit to actually weigh several ectoplasmic bodies. Sir William found that their average weight was approximately fifty pounds. On several occasions this man of science saw the ectoplasmic mass take on various human shapes, which would then walk around the dimly lighted room and speak to various persons present. Sir William also mentions that these solid entities even debated loudly and hotly with him and others on various topics! Full details regarding such dark wonders can be found in Gambier Bolton's book *Ghosts In Solid Form.*[7]

Not only are such weird happenings to be found in spiritualist circles, but they also occur in witchcraft ceremonies. Usually this dark ritual is reserved for a sabbath when a full complement of witches is present. It is said that the best time to work such a demonstration of necromancy is on the Feast of the Dead, or Halloween, which is one of the four great sabbaths. Apparently other witches present act as energy amplifiers, thus making it easier to conjure forth spirits with solid form.

The most ghastly form of necromancy is the calling up of spirits in their dead physical bodies. There are numerous accounts of sorcerers performing this gruesome rite at tombs and graveyards. We know, of course, that the dead cannot return. What really happens in this profane rite is that a demon takes possession of the corpse being used; an unholy force then activates the cadaver, causing it to speak and answer questions.

Impossible? The Bible tells us in no uncertain terms that Satan is capable of performing lying signs and wonders. What mortal man knows the extent of Satan's power? If the devil has power, as the Bible states, "to give *life* unto the image of the beast, that the image of the beast should both *speak,* and cause that as many as would not worship the image of the beast should be killed" (Rev. 13:15), believe me, the Evil One has the power to speak through a rotting corpse!

During the time of Moses, the magicians at Pharaoh's court turned their rods into serpents by Satanic means. Using

[7] (London: W. Rider, 1971).

their occult powers, they even duplicated several of the miracles Moses had performed. Christians are told in the Bible not to be ignorant concerning the devices of Satan. We know the devil has power; yet it is limited power. God's power is unlimited, and Jesus is *always* victor, in any test of strength between the two.

Martin Luther called Satan "the ape of God" because he is forever busy trying to imitate divine wonders and miracles. Necromancy is Satan's brazen attempt at imitating the resurrection of the dead. We know that the human spirit activates our body and gives it life and movement. When death comes, the human spirit leaves its mortal frame, and nothing remains but a corpse. Since it is a spirit, albeit our human spirit, which gives the human body movement and propulsion, is it so difficult to believe that another spirit (if given permission) could likewise for a moment of time reanimate that dead body and make it move or speak? Demons are not allowed on their own to possess a corpse. However, if some witch invokes an evil spirit for such a purpose, then the demon conjured up is no longer under divine restriction, for he has been summoned by human agency to perform a sacrilege; hence the blame for this heinous sin must fall upon the witch.

In his book, *The Magic Island*, American anthropologist and occultist William Seabrook tells us of some things he discovered while investigating voodoo in the West Indies, particularly Haiti. He mentions the terrifying Baron Samedi, whom voodoo practitioners acknowledge as the spirit of graveyards and zombies. When voodoo cult members need a corpse for their black ceremonies, they go to a country graveyard at midnight, and select a wooden cross. On top of the cross is placed a silk top hat, and around its arms they drape a frock coat. Three lighted candles are then placed at the foot of the cross.

The necromancers, bearing gifts of food and liquor, kneel down before the "image" they have made and knock together two stones. This is done to awaken Baron Samedi, dreaded lord of graveyards. Upon being invoked by the Voodoo worshipers, the frightening Baron Samedi makes his presence known and felt.

On some occasions there may be no materialization of the spirit being conjured up. However, the cross dressed as a figure will signal the seekers that Baron Samedi is present and gives his approval to proceed. While the necromancers are genuflecting and beseeching the dark lord of graveyards to assist them, suddenly the long coattails will begin flapping, and the black top hat will be pushed back and forth by invisible hands. At other times, Baron Samedi will materialize and show himself to the necromancers. Those who have seen him report that his appearance is enough to make one's blood run cold. It is said that while the invokers are carrying out their unholy ritual, a tall black man with eyeless sockets in his head will appear and stare at them!

Once Baron Samedi makes his presence known, phase two of the necromantic rite begins, the digging up of the required corpse. The sorcerer puts his question to the dead body, and like an unholy ventriloquist's dummy, the cadaver answers him in a low hollow voice. Warning is given that only those with strong nerves should attempt this occult operation. Backing out at any stage of the aforesaid demonic ceremony, once it is begun, brings the wrath of hell down upon the frightened person's head.

Writing on this theme in 1929, William Seabrook also makes mention of General Benoit Batraville, a commander of the revolutionary forces in Haiti. In the year 1920, the general was shot dead in an ambush. Those who searched his body found a notebook containing secret incantations for conjuring forth the dead, all written in the general's own handwriting. One of these rites had to do with European diabolism.

The sorcerer was to enter a graveyard at midnight carrying a loaded rifle. Upon selecting a grave, he would fire the rifle three times. After each shot, he would shout forth in a loud voice, "In the name of Astaroth, I require of you who are dead that you come to me." The general wrote, "You will hear a stormy noise, but do not take fright—fire a shot. Spirits of the dead will materialize and appear to you; *you must not run away,* but walk backwards three steps, saying these words: 'I besprinkle you with incense and myrrh such as perfumed Astaroth's tomb.' At this point, stated the general, you ask the dead to reveal the future. We find in medieval demonology that Astaroth was the demon who knew all secrets. The general states that to "lay the spirits again," one must throw a handful of graveyard dirt to the "four corners of the earth." The sorcerer then dismisses the dead with these words: "Go back from whence you came, from dirt you were created, to dirt you may return. Amen."

One of the most terrifying descriptions of necromancy ever recorded is given by Lucan in his *Pharsalia.* Sextus, the son of the famous Roman general, Pompei the Great, was most anxious to find out whether or not his father would defeat Caesar in battle. When he could not obtain a clear and definite answer as to the outcome of the war from the oracles, he summoned up his courage and decided to seek out a powerful witch by the name of Erichtho. If ever there was a person sold out completely to the devil, it was Erichtho. Lucan wrote that this daughter of Satan surrounded herself with the vileness and stench of death. She deliberately chose to live

among the tombs, sleeping in a tomb as though she were a
corpse. Erichtho filled her apartment-tomb with ugly objects
of death—funeral shrouds, charred human bones, eyeballs,
tongues, and testicles that she had stolen from corpses recently buried.

Upon approaching Erichtho's eerie residence, Sextus met
her and asked his question. He was told by the witch that
only the dead could answer him, so they both must go to a
battlefield near at hand and obtain the body of a soldier recently killed in battle. Sextus agreed to go through with the
gruesome rite. Reaching the battlefield, they groped around
for some time among the mangled bodies of dead soldiers.

Finally they obtained a suitable corpse, one that had its
lungs, tongue, and larynx still intact. Making their way back
to the witch's lair, they laid the body, with its gaping wounds
and congealed blood, on a cold marble slab. The witch then
made a brew consisting of saliva from a mad dog, the skin of
a reptile, the flesh of a wild hyena that has feasted on dead
human bodies, poisonous herbs, and menstrual blood. While
the witch heated this concoction, Sextus was ordered to cut a
hole in the corpse just above its heart. When it had been
done, Erichtho poured the putrid brew into the gaping hole.

After this stomach-turning performance, the witch called
upon the demons of hell, reminding the evil powers of her
faithfulness and devotion to them. In her conjuration ceremony, proud mention was made of other hair-raising horrors
and sacrilegious rites performed. Then the atmosphere became charged with foreboding and dread. Sextus was terrified almost into insanity, and a sinister chill crept over his
flesh. When Erichtho concluded her invocation to the infernal powers, a clap of thunder reverberated through the dank
musty tomb. As demon spirits were summoned forth from
the dark abyss, there was heard the fearful roaring of wild

beasts and the hissing of snakes. Suddenly the corpse came
to its feet, and through cracked and blood-crusted lips foretold the defeat of General Pompei's armies. When the prophecy was completed, Erichtho dismissed the evil spirit and
burned the corpse.

> From dead men's lips
> Scarce cold, in fuller accents falls the voice;
> Not from some mummied frame in accents shrill
> Uncertain to the ear.[8]

FORTUNE-TELLING

Innumerable cases are on record proving conclusively that
genuine fortune-telling (sometimes called second-sight, clairvoyance, or prevision) does exist. One indisputable source
that backs up this claim is the Bible. We find in Acts 16:16
that the apostle Paul meets a fortune-telling damsel, "which
brought her masters much gain by soothsaying." The account relates that she followed Paul and Silas around saying,
"These men are the servants of the most high God, which
shew unto us the way of salvation" (Acts 16:17).

Demons will quite often tell the truth, if it is in their interest to do so. Confusion would have resulted if Paul had allowed the fortune-telling python spirit to go unchallenged.
Undoubtedly many people were led to believe that the clairvoyant damsel was highly favored by heaven. After all, she
did have a remarkable fortune-telling gift. What really con-
fused matters (Satan is the author of confusion) was her constant announcement that Paul and Silas were servants of the
most high God. Since the damsel had supernatural insight
concerning the spiritual status of these men, people would

[8] *The Pharsalia of Lucan*, 2nd. ed. (London, 1870), p. 179.

quite naturally assume that she was controlled by the same spiritual power as these two servants of God.

Paul wanted to dislodge any such false notion. It is written, "What concord hath Christ with Belial?" (II Cor. 6:15). Being grieved in his spirit concerning the confusion being wrought by this fortune-telling maiden, Paul commanded the evil python spirit in the name of Christ to come out of her. By Christ's power, the young woman was set free and delivered. The Bible tells us that her masters became furious when they "saw that the hope of their gains was gone" (Acts 16:19). For their good deed, Paul and Silas were thrown into jail and beaten. At midnight, these two servants of God begin to sing praises unto the Lord. While they were singing, something cataclysmic happened. Listen to the biblical account of what occurred:

> And suddenly there was a great earthquake, so that the foundations of the prison were shaken; and immediately all the doors were opened, and every one's bands were loosed. And the keeper of the prison awaking out of his sleep, and seeing the prison doors open, he drew out his sword, and would have killed himself, supposing that the prisoners had been fled. But Paul cried with a loud voice, saying, Do thyself no harm: for we are all here. Then he called for a light, and sprang in, and came trembling, and fell down before Paul and Silas, And brought them out, and said, Sirs, what must I do to be saved? And they said, Believe on the Lord Jesus Christ, and thou shalt be saved, and thy house. And they spake unto him the word of the Lord, and to all that were in his house. And he took them the same hour of the night, and washed their stripes, and was baptized, he and all his, straightway. (Acts 16:26–33)

In this wonderful narrative, we are clearly told that clairvoyant powers come from evil spirits. It is also shown that dedicated Christians can take authority over soothsaying demons and cast them out in the name of Christ. More wonderful still, sinners can be saved by believing in the name of our Lord Jesus Christ. This portion of Scripture has something for saint, sinner, and occultist.

ASTROLOGY

Astrology has mushroomed into big business today. Scores of horoscope books are written each year, and some have sold two and three million copies. There are astrology books for gamblers, teenagers, swingers, good health, dieters, cooking, investors, and even for pet owners. It is estimated that the United States now has some 1200 newspapers which carry daily horoscope columns, and pity the editor who should ever inadvertently omit one. Interest in astrology has grown so great that certain large business firms have even taken to employing full-time astrologers.

The more sophisticated astrologers usually soothe clients by telling them that their astrological chart clearly shows they have positive character traits. The one who seeks out an astrologer is very often told that he or she has a warm, kind, and sensitive nature. One can imagine how such an analysis would feed a starved ego. The inquirer may be told that his horoscope shows "anything of a fundamental nature can be handled well today." Those born under the sign of Capricorn, for example, are warned to "avoid arguments on February 20." It is also suggested that Sagittarians "avoid social contact on February 20." Scorpio is reminded that her horoscope for February 20 reads, "Have fun with congenials in the evening." Pisces is given this piece of sage advice: "Stop being so much to yourself and get out socially where you can have a good time, meet interesting people."

One can see from such conglomerate nonsense that the horoscope-caster is playing it safe. This is the kind of hollow, meaningless prediction astrologers usually palm off upon credulous people. On the surface, such prognostications may appear harmless and even somewhat amusing; nevertheless, as one begins to pattern his decisions and life by the horoscope, strange things often do start to happen. Many of the events and happenings predicted in that particular person's horoscope *begin to come true.* (This is especially true when a detailed horoscope has been cast for someone.) With each passing day, our horoscope user becomes more convinced that there really is something to astrology. He knows that many things of a personal nature in his detailed horoscope have come true. Reason tells him that this could not possibly be coincidence. The overwhelming evidence of fulfilled horoscope predictions convinces him that the future *can* be known through astrology. Thus another poor soul falls prey to what Martin Luther called "the subtle foolery of astrology."

If there is nothing to astrology, how is it that a person's horoscope can come true even in the small matters? The answer is jolting, to say the least. The real reason a person's horoscope comes true is because demons make it come true. Behind the scenes, demonic forces begin to manipulate events and circumstances in order that things predicted in a person's horoscope might come to pass. The life of the horoscope user, unbeknownst to himself, gradually becomes controlled by demons.

Hence, astrology is actually just another fortune-telling art. It should be remembered that serious psychic disturbances have been known to afflict those who practice astrology. Let all those who traffic in astrology heed the following scriptural warning:

Let now the astrologers, the stargazers, the monthly prognosticators, stand up, and save thee from these things that shall come upon thee. Behold, they shall be as stubble; the fire shall burn them; they shall not deliver themselves from the power of the flame. (Isa. 47:13–14)

According to today's astrologers, our world is just beginning to enter the Aquarian Age. This is supposed to be "an airy sign that will influence people toward aspiration and faith." It was the highly successful Broadway musical called *Hair* that popularized the following song about astrology:

> When the moon is in the Seventh House
> And Jupiter aligns with Mars
> Then peace will guide the planets
> And love will steer the stars.

In 1970, radio stations all across the land were playing this song from *Hair* that gives astrology a glamorous image. There is no doubt that many young people have been led into astrology by such songs. If they only knew what really makes astrology work, many would recoil in horror.

One noted astrologer has observed that today's young people "are interested in astrology because they've found the material things failing them, and they're trying to find their souls." But the Word of God comes forcefully to mind here: "There is a way which seemeth right unto a man, but the end thereof are the ways of death" (Prov. 14:12).

9.

Divination Explained

■ How does soothsaying work? What power can possibly dredge up hidden secrets of the past? How can future events be foretold when they haven't happened yet? These are some of the perplexing questions one must face in studying occultism.

We all know that time has three dimensions—past, present, and future. To begin, let us consider divination in conjunction with time past. By what means can hidden secrets of the past be revealed? There are countless instances on record where two persons were the only ones who knew a certain secret; one of them dies and the other person goes to a spiritualist meeting, perhaps for the first time. It may well be he is a little skeptical about the whole thing. Reasoning in his heart, he says, "How can the dead come back and communicate with the living?" Humbug! Suddenly his eyes widen with wonderment, and the hackles come up on his neck. He can hardly believe his ears! He is actually being told a secret that only he and his departed wife knew. No one else in the whole wide world knew of it. Being a logical person, he reasons that the message revealed to him just has to be from his departed wife. How could it be otherwise? And so another skeptic has been turned into a confirmed spiritualist or occultist.

What is the real explanation behind such mystical happenings? Most mediums honestly believe their "spirit guides" are able to make contact with the departed dead. It is said that the controlling spirit often reveals a secret supposedly given to him by some departed soul, who wishes to let the living spouse know that all is well and beautiful in the spirit summer land.

Advanced occultists, however, have a different explanation. They tell us that on the higher astral planes there exist what are called "the Akashic Records," sometimes referred to as "the records of the astral light." These mystical records are said to contain all events and happenings that have ever occurred since the beginning of time. Everything all persons have ever seen, said, or done up to the present time are, according to occultists, in the Akashic Records.

What happens is that dedicated occultists are taken in spirit to these higher astral realms and are shown records of various lives. In this way they are able to tell all about a person's past and present life. What takes place in a spiritualist meeting, unbeknown to mediums, is that the possessing spirit—a demon—also has access to the Akashic Records.

There are several accounts in Holy Writ which indicate that Satan has an amazingly complete record of all of our lives. Take, for example, the startling incident of "the seven sons of Sceva." We are told in Acts 19 that there were certain Jewish exorcists, seven in number, who attempted to cast an evil spirit out of a man in the name of Christ:

And the evil spirit answered and said, Jesus I know, and Paul I know; but who are ye? And the man in whom the evil spirit was leaped on them, and overcame them, and prevailed against them, so that they fled out of the house naked and wounded. And this was known to all the Jews and Greeks also dwelling at Ephesus; and fear fell on them all, and the name of Jesus was magnified. And many that believed came, and confessed, and shewed their deeds. Many of them also which used *curious arts* [magical arts] brought their books together, and burned them before all men: and they counted the price of them, and found it fifty thousand pieces of silver. So mightily grew the word of God and prevailed. (Acts 19:15–20)

Notice that the evil spirit mentioned in our text *knew* Christ and Paul. Moreover, the demon was well aware that the seven men, who were trying to cast him out, were not servants of God. How did the demon know such facts? The demon had access to Satan's records which listed the past deeds, sins, and spiritual condition of these men. Another text corroborating the claim that Satan keeps a record of all our lives reads as follows:

And the great dragon was cast out, that old serpent, called the Devil, and Satan, which deceiveth the whole world: he was cast out into the earth, and his angels were cast out with him. And I heard a loud voice saying in Heaven, Now is come salvation, and strength, and the kingdom of our God, and the power of his Christ: For the accuser of our brethren is cast down, which accused them before our God day and night. (Rev. 12:9–10)

In order for Satan to accuse Christians before God day and night, he would have to have precise knowledge of our sins and failures. The text under discussion here is fraught with meaning. Picture the awful tenacity of Satan, "the accuser of our brethren." He has the evidence against us; make no mistake about it. But while he roars forth our mistakes, sins, and failures to God, suddenly there appears one like unto the Son of Man, clothed with a vesture *dipped in blood*; yea His name is called the Word of God. "And one shall say unto Him, What are these wounds in thine hands? Then he shall answer, Those with which I was wounded in the house of my friends" (Zech. 13:6).

Some weary pilgrim along life's road is having a bad time of it. He has been tossed to and fro and is constantly buffeted by the enemy of his soul. The trials and pressures of life are proving too much for him and beginning to take their toll. See that battered brother as he faces the rage and fury of one emotional storm after the other. All the powers of hell seem to have been unleashed against him, in an attempt to crush him.

The arch demon who masterminded "Operation Downfall" exclaims to his cohorts: "Ha, we have him now! Look, the stalwart Christian is stumbling—now he is falling! Look at him lying on the side of life's road, beaten, bloodied, and bruised." And a rattling cheer issues forth from the netherworld.

Swifter than the black wings of night, news of this victory is relayed to hell's infernal prince. The whole demon realm is jubilant. Wild, unearthly laughter rends the air of that nightmarish world. The domain of devils waves its black banner in triumph. From that abode of dread can be heard the cry of demon lords, "One of heaven's own has fallen prey to us!" echoing and re-echoing through the caverns of the damned.

Satan is quick to claim his booty. Soaring to the realms of resplendent light and glory, he approaches heaven's gate. He demands an audience with His august Majesty, the God of heaven and earth, and because his appointed position is that of accuser, the request is granted. Boldly the slanderer presents his case against one of Christ's lambs, insisting that divine justice issue a verdict of eternal death against the fallen

Christian. With a slow smile, Satan reminds the heavenly court of its own holy law, "The soul that sinneth, it shall die" (Ezek. 18:4).

In growing rage, Satan demands that the backslider be punished to the full extent of God's law. A holy hush falls over the court of inquiry. Behold, the sinner's friend and advocate now approaches. Divine Justice is reminded that the One standing before them has suffered and died for the accused. Proof of this fact is given by Christ Himself when He declares, "Behold my hands and my feet . . ." (Luke 24:39). The scars in our Lord's hands, feet, and side are tokens of His great love for lost humanity.

Every Christian should rejoice in the biblical declaration, "Wherefore he is able to save them to the uttermost that come unto God by him, seeing *he ever liveth to make intercession for them*" (Heb. 7:25). Friend, do you get what it says here? The devil cannot stand Christ's divine intervention on our behalf. He is forced to slink away from the presence of such tender love and concern. To the one who has stumbled and fallen along the way, our Savior now comes through the power of His Word. Lovingly our Lord invites him to confess his mistakes and failures. There are no words to describe the tenderness of God toward a penitent sinner. One can detect the beat of God's great heart of love in these passages of Scripture: "A broken and a contrite heart, O God, thou wilt not despise" (Ps. 51:17). Again we read, "If we confess our sins, he is faithful and just to forgive us our sins, and to cleanse us from all unrighteousness" (I John 1:9). We can only gaze in wonder at the provision God has made for sinful man. As the hymn writer expressed it:

> O the love that drew salvation's plan
> O the grace that brought it down to man
> O the mighty gulf that God did span
> At Calvary.

We have seen how clairvoyants can tell both the past and present by tuning in to the higher astral planes and reading the so-called Akashic Records. Reading the future, however, is a different matter. Since the future has not yet occurred, events connected with future time are not in the Akashic Records. It is only when the future becomes the present that happenings connected with this aspect of time can be recorded. If such be the case, then how do occultists foretell the future?

We might begin this aspect of our study by considering the law of probability. There is an old adage that "coming events cast their shadows before them." A person may have several alternative courses open before him. Once he makes a decision, that person has to go through with his decision and accept the consequences. In many cases, the individual, by his choice, may be forced to go a long time on the path he has chosen until an opportunity presents itself for him to make a change.

It is basically true that man is master of his own destiny. Yet the average person has so little willpower that he allows the circumstances of life to mold him into something other than what he wants to be. Since this is the case with most people, a clever fortune-teller can predict with some certainty the future life of such individuals.

With the man who is truly "master of his fate," a considerable difference exists. It is really this man's inner strength that determines his course in life, and so, to know his inner strengths is to have a pretty good idea of where he's going. In both cases, it is not fortune-telling but rather an appraisal of character.

It is the writer's opinion that most fortune-tellers are far better psychologists than they are soothsayers. Genuine fortune-telling powers are not all that easy to obtain. It takes a lot of hard work, dedication, sacrifice, and most of all, a tenacity of purpose to become a powerful psychic. The average shopworn fortune-teller will make predictions based on information artfully extracted from her client. The best that such powerless fortune-tellers can hope for is that the law of probability will work out in their favor.

When genuine fortune-telling powers are operative, behind the scenes, hosts of demon spirits are influencing untold numbers of people to commit sin and evil. In many cases, people are drawn into the path of evil by their own selfish lusts. We read in Scripture that "the whole world lieth in wickedness" (I John 5:19). Some persons are more controlled by evil influences than others. There are those in our sick society who have committed the foulest of crimes. The only reason they can give for their wicked actions: a voice told them to do it! Others confess that an overwhelming compulsion takes control of their minds and hypnotically forces them to commit some dastardly act.

One teenage girl who had used drugs told me that she was baby-sitting one day with her brother's two children. Suddenly a gripping compulsion came over her to throw the children into the fireplace. She became terribly frightened as the compelling force grew stronger and threatened to completely possess her. Hysterical with fear, she ran out of the house. Several blocks away she came to her senses and phoned her brother and his wife to come home immediately. She told the writer that no one really understood her problem. Several times in our conversation she asked, "What was it that tried to make me do such a terrible thing?"

Discerning individuals are becoming increasingly aware that in our present permissive society great numbers of people are now controlled by evil spirits, in various degrees. This

brings us to the crux of our question: certain occult teaching
has it that there is an astral plane where past, present, and future time all exist simultaneously. They teach that this high
astral plane contains a reflection of the Great Universal
Mind. Advanced occultists are supposedly able to penetrate
this astral realm and see reflections of future events.

Theoretically, this is how, from the occult view, all fortune-
telling, prevision, and second sight is done. The writer does
not accept their claim. It may be that God does permit Satan
a limited glimpse into the future from time to time, and that
he in turn passes this information along to a possessing
demon, thus aping the spiritual gift of prophecy, but no mere
mortal has ever been given the ability to read the future. In
the words of our Lord Jesus Christ, "It is not for you to know
the times or the seasons, which the Father hath put in his
own power" (Acts 1:7).

It is a master-stroke of evil genius the different ways Satan
makes it appear that psychics, clairvoyants, mediums, and all
soothsayers can tell the future. For not only do the Akashic
Records exist, but another journal is kept of every person's
thought life! Since Satan is "the accuser of mankind," it
would be mandatory for him as well as God to keep a record
of all our deeds and thoughts.

It has been said that thought is parent to the deed. We
know that demons influence men to commit sin and wickedness by tempting them with evil thoughts. Once a person
yields in his mind to some evil suggestion, it is recorded both
by heaven and hell. Whether a person actually commits the
deed does not alter the fact that he has sinned *in his heart.*
Jesus taught this truth when He declared, "Whosoever look-
eth on a woman to lust after her hath committed adultery
with her already in his heart" (Matt. 5:28).

Most events and happenings in life are thought out before enacted. Possibly there may be a considerable lapse of time before the evil thoughts in men's hearts are carried out to fruition, and in many cases, divine intervention or cowardice on the sinner's part will stop certain wicked thoughts from becoming wicked deeds.

All tuned-in soothsayers, regardless of whether they read tea leaves, Tarot cards, the crystal ball, or the palm, usually have a strange power come over them at the moment of fortune-telling. What happens is that another spirit takes control, and the fortune-teller says things of which she has no knowledge herself.

People who go to fortune-tellers, clairvoyants, mediums, astrologers, or who dabble in other occult practices are unknowingly opening themselves up to demon influence. We should never forget that demonic spirits have but one desire; to ruin and damn the souls of men. Day after day these evil harvesters garner data about each one of us. All such information is placed into Satanic dossiers. The messengers of Satan now have access to all the accumulated information that has been gathered concerning our personal lives. Even the secret sinful thoughts of men's hearts are known to them.

Behind the scenes, infernal strategists from the Order of Thrones take this information and use it to work out various combination-plays in the lives of people. What we are suggesting here may seem farfetched to some. But I remind the reader that in the Book of Job we are told this actually does happen. You will recall that the devil was allowed to work out a series of happenings in the life of Job diabolically calculated to make him fall into ruin and defeat. Job came through with flying colors, and God richly blessed him. Does the reader seriously believe that Job is the only one whom Satan has drawn up elaborate plans to ruin?

Your soul is of such great value that the devil has ordered his master strategists to work out various schemes that will cause you to fall into sin and hell. When each plot against you is concocted, then Satan dispatches a legion of demons to carry it out. If it so happens that a person is spiritually strong enough to resist the alluring bait on the dangling Satanic hook, then more subtle ways will be found to attempt to break him. The only hope man has is in Christ. When the wily emissaries of hell are drafting their plans for your downfall, every weakness you have is carefully considered and exploited. Their evil genius is such that they know just where and how to apply the exact amount of pressure to ruin each life.

There are people who have had dramatic upheavals in their lives—sickness, accident, financial loss, marital breakup, madness, and even death—after just one seance session, or even after a chance visit to some fortune-teller. Such experiences can be likened to a curious fish inspecting a worm on a hook—the controller at the other end of the line has only one motive in mind—to get that fish into his frying pan! Although occasionally a fish does manage to wriggle off the hook and escape with its life, yet it will be scarred by the encounter.

Years ago, a young woman, sister of a Christian friend of mine, was persuaded by another woman, who worked in the same office, to visit a fortune-teller. Not really believing in such things, Miss A went along out of courtesy. Miss A's skepticism concerning occultism was challenged and shaken when the fortune-teller said to her, "You had a brother who died recently!" A number of other personal things were also told her that no one was supposed to know.

Some time later, Miss A was invited to a house party given by the lady who had invited her to visit the fortune-teller. While at the party, Miss A was seized with an unexplainable compelling urge to give a certain message to her hostess. Unable to resist the overwhelming compulsion, she spoke forth in ecstatic tones the message that had come upon her. After delivering her message, she felt a great sense of relief and joy. Suddenly, to the amazement of everyone there, and more so to Miss A herself, she began to sing in a beautiful voice. Normally, the young woman couldn't sing a note!

Somewhat stunned and frightened by the incident Miss A sought out another office employee who was involved in spiritualism. Miss A asked her, "Should I continue to go along with these mystical impulses, or would it be best to resist them?" The other woman replied, "By all means break away from it—if you can! I wish it were possible for me to quit the whole damnable thing, but I've been involved so long with occultism that it's really too late for me." Then she proceeded to tell Miss A about a successful businessman who had delved deeply into occultism. His tampering with the mystical arts had brought him to a state of hysteria and near mental collapse. Spirits were constantly hounding the poor man, giving him no rest day or night.

Since her one brush with occultism, the Christian man's sister has had a very unhappy life. A whole series of unfortunate incidents have dogged her steps. Although Miss A has heard the gospel message from her brother, yet she has not been able to yield her heart to Christ. She would really like to accept Christ, but something keeps holding her back!

We are aware that many occultists will say they have practiced the mystical arts for years and nothing drastic has happened to them. It must be pointed out that some spirits are more wicked and demanding than others. Christ tells us about the unclean spirit who returns with "seven other spirits more wicked than himself . . . and the last state of that man is worse than the first" (Matt. 12:45).

Certain evil spirits will use the subtle approach in dealing with their victims; others are more direct, harsh, and cruel. Spirits who manifest their presence and power in occult circles all have the same overwhelming ambition: to deceive and beguile those who seek them. It can be said that the practicing occultist has relative peace and freedom, providing he obeys the whims and demands of his spirit guide.

But, just let that person attempt to break free of his spirit control and see what happens. His whole life-style will take on a negative reaction. Unusual things will start occurring in his life, bringing him bad luck and misfortune. It is as if spirits keep their victims on a kind of psychic leash, and if for some reason they are disobedient, or if they try to escape from the psychic influence controlling their lives, then the leash is tightened around their necks. Only Christ has the power to set these captives free.

10.

Witchcraft

■ A tidal wave of interest in witchcraft is sweeping the world today. Untold numbers of young people are experimenting with witchcraft and actually practicing soul-destroying magical rites. It is reported that in England alone there are presently some 30,000 practicing witches.[1] Reporter Dan L. Thraff in Los Angeles states, "In France, 60,000 sorcerers are taking in $200 million a year for 'healing the sick' and restoring sexual prowess. Enterprising spiritualists and witches along the Mexican border charged American parents $400 to "protect" their soldier sons in Vietnam.

Los Angeles has an official County Witch, a title ceremoniously bestowed upon Mrs. Louise Huebner by the county supervisor. Witch Huebner made her official debut in July 1968 at the famed Hollywood Bowl. All who attended were given red candles, chalk, and garlic. Midway through the meeting, Witch Huebner instructed everyone who wanted to be rejuvenated sexually to repeat the following chant after her three times:

[1] *Christianity Today*, March 26, 1971.

Light the flame
Bright the fire
Red the color of desire.

Numbers of middle-age persons in the audience have reported they did experience a new surge of sexual power.[2]

Californians are becoming more concerned with each passing year as witchcraft, black magic, and Satanism continue to grow at an alarming rate. In the Los Angeles *Herald-Examiner*, December 21, 1969, mention is made that groups of hippies all over the state are holding witchcraft discussions. Animals, particularly dogs, are being sacrificed, and there are fire-walking and blood-drinking ceremonies being carried out. It is also reported that in the initiation ceremonies, participants are required to eat the entrails of an animal while its heart is still beating.

It may seem paradoxical, but witches do not always agree with each other. There is a difference of opinion among them as to the source of witchcraft power. Many witches, wizards, and warlocks do not believe in the existence of either God or Satan. Dame Huebner declared, "There is no such thing as black magic and white magic, evil spirits and good spirits . . . there is only *energy!*" The infamous Anton La Vey, High Priest of the First Church of Satan, expresses a similar sentiment:

La Vey says he does not worship Satan, or even believe in his existence. "But there is a force—a Godhead or whatever you want to call it. It is a displacement of the energy of human beings that will become a malleable source of action for the magician—the witch." [3]

[2] *Time* magazine, March 21, 1969.
[3] *Look* magazine, August 24, 1971.

This ingenious theory holds that all occult powers are inanimate by nature and have nothing whatever to do with either God or Satan. Down through the centuries, many witches and sorcerers considered God and Satan as merely symbols of power, with no real existence as personalities. The parallel is drawn by those who cling to this view that all occult powers are similar in essence to electricity, which has no personality and is therefore inanimate. The point is then made that certain men have discovered how to harness electricity and make it do their bidding. Proceeding a step further, they will tell you that electricity can be used for either good or evil purposes. It can be made to heat a room, cook food, or banish the darkness of night. The same force can also be used to electrocute a person! Similarly, witches and sorcerers claim to have learned how to harness the hidden astral forces; by performing certain ceremonies and rituals, they can make these mysterious powers do their bidding.

There is one major flaw in this theory: they have overlooked the basic law of cause and effect. For every effect, there has to be a cause. The reason electricity behaves as it does is because some Intelligence placed that power in the universe. Anything indicative of design and order must of necessity have an intelligence behind it. Once we accept this truth, then we are compelled to believe there has to be some kind of intelligence behind all occult powers.

It is really a lust for power that drives the witch ever deeper into the mysteries of occultism. The ultimate aim in witchcraft was summed up by the serpent: "Ye shall not surely die: For God doth know that in the day ye eat thereof, then your eyes shall be opened *and ye shall be as gods,* knowing good and evil" (Gen. 3:4–5).

The consuming passion of every sorcerer is to harness the power of the spheres and to ultimately make himself a god.

To succeed in their proud, Satanic ambition they must experience to the full all that life and death has to offer. Not only is it required of them to have personal knowledge of everything in the universe, but all things in realms of light and darkness have to be mastered and brought under their control. The great depths of both good and evil have to be plumbed and everything contained therein thoroughly understood.

The Bible declares that "man is made in the image of God." Occultists who do believe in a personal God and devil take this to mean that man is God in miniature form. It is claimed that through mysticism, man can release his dormant psychic powers and extend his influence to all realms, both terrestrial and celestial, eventually becoming a master or god. Such magicians consider the universe to be a mighty cosmic ocean with tremendous astral currents flowing through it. These currents are said to flow through all matter, space, and time. The constant ebbing and swelling of great cosmic tides throughout the vasty deeps are considered to be the very powers holding the universe together. Through proper occult wisdom and knowledge, it is claimed that man can tune in to these great cosmic powers and harness them to obey his will.

Various secret occult societies maintain they can teach you how to tap the great universal flow of cosmic energy. In order to acquire such occult powers, one must be willing to perform certain ceremonies and rites. The purpose behind ceremonial initiation rites is to please the so-called astral gods who control these mystical powers. If the acolyte continues in the way and does all he can to please the controlling astral gods and spirits, then he can draw upon this cosmic energy and eventually become a witch of power.

Occultists are basically divided into two distinct factions, those who do believe in a personal devil and those who simply personify the force of evil and acknowledge it to be the devil or Satan. Occultists who believe in a personal devil accept the traditional view of demons being fallen angels. On the other hand, those occultists who merely personify evil and acknowledge this force as Satan believe that demons are merely the spirits of dead wicked men.

Psychic Attacks

In occultism there is also another kind of demon called an "elemental spirit." It is alleged in certain magical circles that such entities are artificially created spirits with a temporary life span. They are mostly used by black magicians to carry out their evil work.

There is an old axiom in spiritualism that "thoughts are living things." What happens is that the magician pictures in his mind a certain type of creature he would like to create. By great concentration and strong willpower, he brings up some hideous form into sharp focus before his mind's eye. It may be a giant toad, a slimy reptile, something semi-human, or half animal, then again it may be a huge slug-like apparition.

Holding this form constant and steady in his mind, the sorcerer then unleashes all his pent-up emotional fury and hatred and sends it into the mental image, thus giving it life. The creature conjured up from the dark deeps of the magician's own evil mind will now go forth to harass and rend some poor victim.

Many psychic attacks are carried out in this manner. There are innumerable cases on record where people have had hair-raising encounters with these terrifying astral creatures.

Coro, Venezuela (Reuters, February 4, 1972)—Police are conducting a ghost-hunt in the village of San Pedro after its 34 inhabitants claimed they are being haunted out of their minds.

Police Chief Ramon Rojas said, "We are going to investigate exhaustively to see if it is true the town is haunted by witches, wizards and demons."

San Pedro's frightened population said ghosts first appeared at midnight New Year's Eve. Among them were said to be "a fat woman accompanied by *enormous man-eating animals* and a dwarf who burns his victims sadistically. . . ."

One resident, Maria Acosta de Dias, claims: "The fat woman tells me every day to commit suicide." Another villager, Martiniano Amaya, says: "The dwarf tries to burn me, I see huge cockroaches and giant insects the dwarf sets on me." Amaya has been so affected by his visions he stays in bed.

In his book, *Jungle Magic*, James H. Neal, Chief Investigations Officer at Accra, Ghana, relates the fearful black magic attacks he suffered in that country. Mr. Neal was sent from London in November, 1952, to take up a new post. At that time Ghana had a serious crime problem which had the authorities badly worried. It became his job to put a stop to the wholesale embezzlement, fraud, and theft being carried out on various government projects.

On several occasions, Chief Officer Neal was threatened with *Ju-ju*, the native form of black magic, because he had arrested certain persons. Being a hard-nosed policeman, he first laughed at the idea. But his skepticism vanished after he experienced his first attack of black magic.

The incident occurred after Chief Officer Neal had been threatened by a man whom he had just arrested. Upon retiring to bed, he felt something nip him on the neck; next he experienced a searing painful sensation in his solar plexus; then a strong invisible force began tugging viciously at his body.

The following nights he was attacked again in the same manner, but this time with more intensity. To quote his own words:

When I actually began to see my attackers, I became very alarmed. . . . These creatures were long-snouted and ugly, and repeatedly attacked my neck and lower body. I could only presume they were on the astral level. During the third night the attacks became increasingly strong. I could see the creatures now very clearly. Artificial entities created by the Ju-ju man and sent to attack me, they were fearsome things. I realized that if this went on much longer I should be dead in the course of a day or two.

After his encounter with these malicious astral entities, Chief Officer Neal was taken to hospital suffering from a strange wasting disease. Doctors held no hope for him. It was only after another powerful Ju-ju man came and performed a white magic ritual that he got better.

An explanation needs to be made here concerning the removing of black magic spells and curses. All genuine adepts of the magical arts have been granted by Satan (whether they are aware of it or not), a certain degree of authority over demon spirits. Evil spirits are compelled by infernal law to obey the magician who is in league with hell, provided that he follows the prescribed ritual to the letter. (But let him make one mistake . . .) The reason behind such a strange transaction is that Satan grants this concession in order to entice people to serve him. There is an old adage which says, "Power corrupts." Nowhere is this statement more true than in occultism. People who are bent on harnessing the dark astral powers eventually become corrupt both morally and spiritually. And the more power they assimilate, the deeper the corruption reaches.

We must remember that there are various orders of demons. Every evil spirit has a certain degree of authority and power, but there are always others more powerful. Consequently, when two sorcerers are engaged in a psychic duel, as in the case of Chief Officer Neal, the one who has the more powerful spirit guide will prevail.

The sorcerer, witch, or juju man who conjures up elemental spirits for black magic purposes thinks that he is the one who actually gives life and impetus to the astral demon. But what really happens is that an evil spirit takes possession of the sorcerer's thought creation. It has been previously mentioned that demons are forbidden by divine law to openly attack just anyone on their own initiative; they must obtain divine permission to do so, and this is seldom granted. Through the human instrumentality of a witch, however, they are relatively free to wreak havoc, terror, and evil upon nearly anyone—except those who are truly Christians.

Master occultist Rollo Ahmed tells us that "thought forms" (elemental spirits) can be built up into any shape and sent out by the sorcerer to do his evil bidding. He states that this power is employed by the black-magic practitioner to cause injury, destruction, immorality, hatred, and strife. The noted occult authority then issues a grave warning:

> But in this form of black magic, as in all others, there is a price to pay, and the time comes when the sorcerer has to deal with the creatures he has created, and only too often they turn upon him to his destruction. (*Black Art*)

Dabbling in black magic can prove very dangerous. One man who is thoroughly convinced of this fact is Serge Kordeiv, a photo-journalist and magazine photographer from Rommey Marsh, Kent, England. Having read a few books on black magic, he decided to investigate it further for the purpose of obtaining material that could be used in a newspaper story.

In order to make the proper connections, Mr. Kordeiv and his wife started going to various night clubs in the Soho and Chelsea districts of London. To whatever new people they met, they always made mention of their interest in black magic. The Kordeiv's were all but ready to give up their investigation, when, quite by accident, they happened to stumble on the real thing.

They tell of being picked up in a chauffeur-driven limousine and taken to a luxurious Victorian house. Upon arriving, the Kordeivs were served drinks and then led through various corridors. At a certain room they were asked to strip and put on small satin aprons. Finally they were escorted to a large room where three walls were draped with heavy red carpeting; on the other wall hung a huge mural depicting "a chained, horned creature overpowering a naked girl amid livid flames."

Just beneath the mural was an altar containing six black candles. We are told that a stark-naked muscular man wearing some kind of hideous devil's mask stood before the altar. Acting as High Priest of Satan, he spoke in a deep voice and asked the other disciples of darkness, all hooded and robed, whether or not these two persons should be allowed to join their black circle. The Kordeivs were aghast when the only reply given was "the plaintive bleating of a goat."

Upon being accepted as disciples of the Prince of Darkness, they were asked to kneel and "swear perpetual homage to Satan." The oath was written out in contract form and signed by them with their own blood. Satan's high priest then formally welcomed this couple into the coven by abruptly placing his hands on their genitals. (Here we have a Satanic mockery of the Christian rite of the laying on of hands to impart spiritual blessing.) The strange thing about this part of the ceremony, report the Kordeivs, was the sudden inexplicable "surge of energy" that went all through them when the obscene hands grabbed their private parts.

After going through the Satanic initiation ritual, Serge Kordeiv found his whole life was dramatically changed. Everything he touched turned to money. Never had he and his wife enjoyed such financial prosperity. But after attending several more meetings, Serge and his wife decided to quit the group.

Two things were responsible for their changed attitude. The coven had performed a Black Mass in which "a wax dummy incorporating nails and hair from the 'outsider' was placed on the altar." (The 'outsider' was a certain prominent businessman whom the group had something against.) A black cock was killed, and each member of the coven had to drink its blood from a chalice. The high priest plunged a knife into the wax image, and blood, or red liquid, gushed out all over a nude girl stretched out on the altar. At the next meeting, Serge and his wife were shocked upon being shown a newspaper telling of the sudden death of the businessman whom they had murdered in effigy. The man had collapsed and died of a heart attack on the same night that they had held a Black Mass for him.

The second thing was that it had come time for them to go through a Satanic confirmation ceremony. This particular rite consisted of sexual acts taking place between the candidate, the high priest, and the coven priestess. Coming to their senses, the Kordeivs decided to break off completely from the group and move to another area.

The Kordeivs soon found that the money they had accumulated since first joining the coven started to quickly go. Every business venture started losing money, and nothing seemed to work out right for them. The most frightening experience of all happened the night they came home and found a monstrous toad sitting on their front step glaring at them. Mrs. Kordeiv became almost hysterical, the toadlike apparition disappeared, and they went into the house. That night both of them woke up with a start. Coming from Mr. Kordeiv's adjoining studio, which had bars on the windows, was "the sound of maniacal laughter—absolutely terrible." The next thing they heard was the loud smashing of glass.

When the first rays of the morning sun shone through their bedroom window, Mr. Kordeiv went downstairs to see what had happened. His studio looked as though a hurricane had struck it. Everything was smashed and in terrible disarray. Even the window bars "had broken under the weight of someone or something bursting out, for the lawn and path were littered with broken glass." [4]

Such was the experience of an unwise couple whose curiosity for black magic dragged them through untold anguish and despair. One cannot just pick up the dark bolts of magical fire and drop them at will without getting burned. There is always a price to pay for use of these forbidden powers, in this world as well as in the world to come.

Master adept L. W. De Laurence spent many years studying and practicing occultism. In the introduction to his *Book of Death and Hindu Spiritism*, he writes that many black magic practitioners in the Orient were able to perform astounding magical feats.

With his own eyes, he actually saw conjurers of the devilish arts make the image of a certain thief appear in their glass. These same sorcerers even demonstrated to him how they could make an old man appear young (but only for the space of two hours and no more). Some of their other magi-

[4] *Man, Myth & Magic*, Issues 31 and 32.

cal accomplishments included the ability to become invisible so that people could not really see them. Evil spirits would divulge to these sorcerers the deepest secrets about people.

De Laurence makes it very clear that all the magical powers demonstrated by such sorcerers came to them after they had made a pact with evil spirits. Once these impious conjurers took this fatal step, they became the dumb, driven slaves of evil spirits. Their whole life was now given over to work havoc, destruction, and evil among all living creatures. In effect, they had to become "devils in the flesh" in order to appease their demonic masters. De Laurence further tells us the awful price these miserable wretches had to pay (in this world): "Ultimately their soul and body was dragged through deep misery. This was all the profit they drew from their diabolical science and damnable magic." [5]

In an old German book written in the last century, a respected physician relates that a certain wealthy farmer came to him one day seeking help. Every night between ten o'clock and midnight he heard weird and mysterious pounding noises in his bedroom that greatly frightened him. No matter what the farmer did, or where he went, these eerie noises constantly haunted him. Under questioning, the farmer admitted there was a bitter disagreement between the village blacksmith and himself over an unpaid debt. The farmer had hired a blacksmith to do some work for him, but upon completion of the job, he refused to pay, maintaining that the work was not satisfactory. His refusal to pay infuriated the blacksmith to such an extent that he threatened the farmer with a "hex."

The physician went to see the blacksmith, and upon meeting this man looked him sternly in the eye and pointedly

[5] L. W. De Laurence, *Book of Death and Hindu Spiritism* (Hackensack, N.J.: Wehman, 1963), p. 20.

asked him, "What do you do every night between ten and twelve o'clock?" Taken aback and shaken by such a significant question, the blacksmith blurted out, "I hammer a bar of iron every night at that time, and all the while I think intently of a bad neighbor of mine who once cheated me out of some money; and I 'will' at the same time that the noise will disturb his rest, until he will pay me back my money to get peace and quiet."

The doctor severely reprimanded the blacksmith, warning him to quit this evil practice immediately. Going to the troubled farmer, he urged him to clear up that old debt and his nocturnal harassment would stop. When the farmer complied with the doctor's wish, he had no more trouble.

Ignorant skeptics and intellectual fools will pooh-pooh such a thing as psychic attack, branding it as superstitious nonsense. But there are simply too many unexplainable cases around to lightly dismiss the matter. French writer C. H. Dewisme described (in *Les Zombis*, 1957) an example of black magic murder that occurred during the occupation of Haiti by American forces after World War 1. He mentions that a *hungan* (voodoo priest) from Port-au-Prince had cast a death spell against an American lieutenant who was put in charge of the police department. The intended victim was told that within one week he would be dead. Being an unbeliever in the supernatural, the lieutenant ridiculed the idea. When the evening of the seventh day arrived, a gendarme came back to the station drunk. While the lieutenant bawled him out, the drunken man took out his gun and shot him dead. Was this merely a coincidence, or did witchcraft cause it to happen?

METHODS OF BLACK MAGIC ATTACK

There are numerous rites and rituals in witchcraft that are expressly intended to cause injury, pain, discomfort, and even death. One method is to produce by incantation an image of the selected victim in a basin of water. Once this has been accomplished, the sorcerer stabs the reflection with a knife. If the spell "works," the water, it is claimed, will turn blood red, and the victim will die. Another way witches hex someone is to take an animal and formally baptize it in the name of their victim. The animal is then cruelly tormented until it dies in agony. While this fiendish rite is being carried out, the witch will work himself up into a terrible rage.

When the evoker of black magic powers reaches that state where his total being is literally charged with hate and malice, he then releases what is called in occultism "a psychic trigger," channeling his ritualized hatred into the tormented dying animal. This current of hate emanating from the witch is easily seen by demons. If the one who performs the ritual of destruction has taken initiation vows to Satan, then demon messengers will carry out the warlock's wish.

Other forms of substitution are also used by the witch, such as making a wax image and baptizing it in the name of him who is to be hexed. Black magic practitioners build their hate and fury up into what is called "a cone of power." When this pyramid of negative energy is fully charged and pulsating, it is then symbolically released by the warlock. We are told that the ritual is even more effective when a coven of witches participates. Sometimes their supercharged "hate force" is directed at a wax doll, who symbolically represents the victim. Caught up in a wild emotional frenzy of hate, the witch will discharge her hellish venom by sticking pins into the wax object while uttering execrable oaths.

Witches have various ways of putting a curse upon someone. One of the most common and time-worn methods used is called "the Black Fast." In this particular ritual, the witch will carefully prepare a delicious meal, after abstaining from all food for two days. After the two days have expired, the witch is very hungry, and her body is crying out for food. Sitting down to a succulent dinner, she will smell the tantalizing aroma of good food, but will refuse to eat one morsel of it!

Her whole body rebels in anger because it is being refused food. This process is calculated to whip up the fiery blood of rage and send it coursing through her veins. The witch has now succeeded in stirring up her psychic currents of hate and revenge. Once this emotional state of wild rage is reached, she throws the meal away and bitterly curses her victim.

After her rage has abated, the witch then sits down and eats a meager meal consisting of two slices of bread, some cheese, and water. The witch must keep repeating this same rite every day for two weeks . . . beginning at the full moon. One can see here the Satanic counterpart to what Jesus said, "This kind [of demon] goeth not out but by prayer and fasting" (Matt. 17:21). Difficult cases in witchcraft can likewise only be magically attacked by cursing and black fasting.

At this point the author feels that he should issue the following warning to all witches, warlocks, and sorcerers. Just in case some who practice the black arts get ideas to hex the writer, I caution them not to give in to the temptation. The author is one who safely abides under the blood of Christ and has a mighty spirit guide protecting him, not some "long-dead Indian chief," but none other than the Holy Spirit of God. It is not our wish that harm should befall those who practice the diabolical arts. Therefore we advise all who may have such a thought in mind to seriously consider *the law of spiritual return.*[6] Calling upon the powers of fire and darkness to hurt one of God's own will only bring the curse you have uttered down upon your own heads.

[6] "The law of return is the principle that the force of a spell which fails, rebounds on the head of the sorcerer" (*The Black Arts*, Richard Cavendish).

11.

Satanism

■ There are people in our society whose driving interest is to really *know* the power of evil. They call themselves Satanists and they are worshipers of a horned god, the goat of Baphomet. These benighted souls practice the worst forms of black magic and have given themselves wholly to the worship of evil and perversion, to the point where they believe that evil is right and good wrong. They wallow in cesspools of moral filth and depravity in devotion to the Prince of Evil. The practice of evil, diabolical evil, is their twisted pleasure.

Satanism is a philosophy of open defiance and rebellion against Almighty God. According to this hellish philosophy, everything that is good, holy, and decent in the world has to be torn down and destroyed. Satanists consider themselves the storm troopers of hell. Their mission in life is to prepare the world for the coming of the Lord Satan!

In our present day, the black raging passions of Satanism are erupting with greater intensity and more regularity than ever before. One shudders to examine the reports of terrible crimes that have been committed by avowed Satanists, not only during the dark ages, but last week.

Down through the centuries there have been spasmodic

outbreaks of Satanism. Consider the infamous La Voisin, sorceress and high priestess of Satan who lived in Paris during the seventeenth century at the time of King Louis XIV. The record tells us that the beautiful but jaded Madame de Montespan, mistress to the king, was fearful that His Royal Highness was losing interest in her. In order to secure her hold on the king, she sought out the sorceress, La Voisin, who told her that in order to obtain Satan's help, a blasphemous ceremony known as the black mass would have to be performed. To give her consent meant that she would have to play a major role in the sacrilegious rite by offering her nude body as an altar.

The celebrant who performed La Voisin's black mass that fateful night was an obscene hunchback named Abbe Guibourg. After the communion elements of bread and wine were consecrated and then defiled in the most debased way imaginable, the renegade priest Guibourg brought forth a tiny baby and held it above the naked body of Madame de Montespan. He then cut the baby's throat with a sharp knife and allowed its blood to gush out over the body of the king's mistress. As the blood splashed over her, she cried out, "Hail, Prince of Darkness! Hear my plea! Let the king's love come only to me."

Acting as Satan's representative, the fat evil hunchback copulated with the king's bloodied mistress. While this defiling act was being performed, all in attendance repeatedly shouted forth, "Hail Satan!"

"Such rites were not for the squeamish," states Gunther Rosenberg, founder and former president of the European Occult Research Society. History informs us that La Voisin confessed to sacrificing some 2,500 babies to Satan as high priestess of this cult. At her trial, she told how young children and babies were purchased for their ceremonies from beggars and prostitutes for a small fee. In her confessions before the courts, she named many of the nobility of that land as her clients. Scores of them fled from France to escape the enraged citizenry and legal prosecution. Upon being found guilty, La Voisin was led to a public square on February 23, 1680, and there burned alive for her monstrous crimes. Thus ended the evil life of the most infamous Satan worshiper in history.

Another notorious Satanist was the Hungarian Countess Elizabeth Báthory. This evil woman was tried and put to death in 1614 when authorities discovered some fifty young girls chained in the dungeon of her castle. Countess Báthory was using the blood of her young victims to bathe in.

The practice of sacrificing innocent children and babies to Satan was not confined to the dark ages; it is being done today. If the present occult craze continues, all the horrors associated with the black mass and Satanism will be revived with frightening implications. So great is the interest in Satanism today that Mercury Records has recorded a black mass in an album entitled "Witchcraft Coven: Destroys Minds & Reaps Souls." Participating Satanists can be heard breaking a crucifix and swearing perpetual allegiance to "our Lord Satan." After a solemn oath to the devil, these words are heard:

If I ever betray my oath, I do now decree to have my throat cut, my tongue and heart torn out . . . and to be buried in the sand of the ocean that the waves of it may carry me away into an eternity of oblivion.

In conclusion, the "high priest" threatens,

If you ever break this oath, we shall pronounce sentence upon you in the name of our Lord Satan . . . that you shall fall into dangerous disease and leprosy, and that in the sign of this vengeance you shall perish by a terrifying and horrible death. . . .

The back of the album jacket declares that to Satanists "the most effective sacrifice is an unbaptized baby." Christian leaders who have heard the album maintain that for sheer vulgarity and blasphemy it has no equal.

Knights Templar

During the Crusades, the Order of the Knights Templar was formed to protect the Holy Sepulcher from the Moslems. Founded in 1118 at Palestine, the Templars became exceedingly wealthy and powerful after several wars with the Saracens. Following their initial prosperity, the Knights Templar degenerated, and confessions revealed that members took part in shocking blasphemies and vile indecencies. French and English adherents of the Templar Order were charged in 1307 with stamping, spitting, and urinating on crucifixes. Those who were initiated into the sect were forced to participate in homosexual acts. The occultist Manly Palmer Hall mentions in his *The Adepts in the Western Tradition* (1949), that "the knights were . . . accused of adoring a curious deity in the form of a monstrous head or a demon in the form of a goat. This idol, named Baphomet, the goat of Mendes, has been called the secret god of the Templars." One of the best-known occultists in the world, Manly Hall maintains that such orders remain with us today and are all part of a "humanist" movement which has continued throughout the centuries and will eventually come together under some such name as "the Invisible Government of the World."

The Hell-Fire Club

A Satanic organization that wielded great political influence in England during the eighteenth century was the notorious Hell-Fire Club. It was founded by a wealthy member of Parliament, Sir Francis Dashwood. According to Daniel P. Mannix's history of that group, *The Hell-Fire Club* (New York, N.Y.: Ballantine Books, 1959), it was "an assocation dedicated to Black Magic, sexual orgies, and political conspiracies. . . ."

Many members of the English chapter of the Hell-Fire Club were influential politicians. Such notable persons as the following were all members of the infamous club: Dashwood, the Chancellor of the Exchequer; the 4th earl of Sandwich, at that time First Lord of the Admiralty; the Earl of Bute, who happened to be the Prime Minister of England; and Thomas Potter, son of the Archbishop of Canterbury, who wrote psalms for their black mass ceremonies. Other members included the Lord Mayor of London, the Prince of Wales, and several of England's greatest artists (including Hogarth) and poets.

We are told that on the Dashwood estate at West Wycombe, some thirty-three miles northwest of London, the Hell-Fire Club members indulged in depraved sexual practices for over twenty years. It is said that Dashwood personally performed black masses over the bodies of naked women, with the express purpose of summoning forth the forces of evil.

Not to be outdone by their Satanic English brothers, the members of the Irish chapter of the Hell-Fire Club spent their lives gambling, drinking, whoring, and blaspheming. They were noted for burning cats alive at their meetings, setting fire to churches, and performing unspeakable atrocities.

A painting by James Worsdale still hangs in Dublin's Natural Gallery showing five members of the infamous Hell-Fire Club of Dublin. Their motto: "Do as you will."

One of the last leaders of the Dublin Hell-Fire Club was a man named Buck Whaley. Upon taking leadership of the club, he swore to "defy God and man in nightly revels." But one day the dissipated young man became remorseful and went to St. Audoen's Church, Dublin, to ask for absolution of his sins. Not being able to locate the minister, he knelt in the darkened nave. He looked up, and lo, he saw the menacing form of Satan himself coming down the aisle toward him! Petrified with fear and gibbering with terror, he ran out of the church.

He fled Ireland and settled on the Isle of Man, to die shortly at age thirty-four, after finishing his memoirs. One can detect a cry of despair from the tortured soul of Buck Whaley as he penned the words, "I feel no trifling sensation from the prospect that this simple narrative may persuade the young and inexperienced, if the language of truth has the power of persuasion, that a life of dissipation can produce no enjoyment, and that tumultuous pleasures afford no real happiness."

MODERN DAY SATANISM IN THE UNITED STATES

It is only fair to point out that most occultists deplore and decry the excesses of Satanists. Yet just as marijuana, perhaps non-addictive of itself, nonetheless creates the psychological dependence that leads to stronger drugs, so all occult groups, by their very existence, are potential incubation centers for the more blatant worshipers of the Lord of Darkness. Many young people today are looking for thrills and kicks. The comparatively "mild" practices of astrology, the I Ching, tarot cards, spiritualism, and white magic soon lose their excitement and appeal for many. At this point such individuals are ready to be led down the left-hand path of occultism—black magic, sorcery, and Satanism.

The black side of occultism is considered the ultimate trip into evil. Self-styled explorers of the unknown who venture into the chilling stream of Satanism soon become trapped by dark astral currents, which wind their way ever downward to the vortex of hell itself. He that hath ears to hear, let him hear: every occult transgression becomes another link in the great chain of darkness that forever binds the soul.

In March, 1970, *Esquire* magazine carried a twenty-six-page feature section devoted to "The Style of Evil" in California. The mushrooming growth of Satanism and witchcraft in that state was given prominent mention. *Esquire*'s Tom Burke described an interview he had with a young female singer from Los Angeles, who claimed to have attended many of the far-out parties held at the Polanski mansion.[1] Describing an occult party held at another place along Sunset Strip, she related how guests "were greeted at the door with a glass of their special hallucinogenic formula." Continuing, she said, "You went in and there were three altars. On two of them, these boys were tied with leather thongs. They were sobbing. These two faggots dressed as nuns—one had a goatee—were beating them with big black rosaries. On the middle altar there was a very young girl. This guy wearing a goat's head had crushed a live frog on her privates. When I came in, he had just cut a little cross on her stomach; not deep, but the party had just started. I don't know how deep the cuts got, because, man, I split from there like Wonder Woman. . . ."

---

[1] Roman Polanski was the husband of slain actress Sharon Tate, who was murdered by Satanists. He had first come to Hollywood to make the controversial film *Rosemary's Baby*. In this horror picture, the leading lady is raped by the devil.

Here is a modern-day version of the black mass. The singer went on to tell what happens to those who start taking daily acid trips: "First you're Christ, then you're Lord of the Underworld." Another of the so-called beautiful people who is said to be hip because he is familiar with the Strip scene knowingly states, "Acid is so spiritual, so, uh, metaphysical, that you are going to be forced into making a choice, between opting for good . . . or tripping with the Lord Satan. That's the whole heavy thing about too many people turned on to acid: to most of them, the devil just looks groovier."

The news media all but ignored the Satanic implements of worship and torture found at the $200,000 home of slain actress Sharon Tate. At the Tate mansion, where five persons were brutally and ritually murdered, were found "black leather masks, whips, ropes and chains—the 'tools' of the Satanic cults." [2]

Before the police apprehended Charles Manson, who had ordered the grisly murders, investigating officers were led through a weird nightmare world of freaked-out long-haired hippies, countless numbers of whom had blown their minds by taking drugs and practicing black magic. As hardened detectives probed ever deeper into the hippie subculture, they were shocked to discover devil worship and perverted sexual orgies that would stagger the minds of normal people. In the haunts of the depraved, they found groups of sadists who worshiped Satan by practicing mutilation ceremonies and even ritual murder before images of Baphomet, a goat-like devil.

In 1963 at Cuidad Victoria, Mexico, federal police made the shocking announcement that Satanists there had sacrificed six persons to demon gods. The record states that

[2] *American Opinion*, September 1970.

hearts had been cut out of living victims during gruesome ceremonies. Others who had fallen into the clutches of this Satanic cult had been killed by stoning on orders from a prostitute-turned-high-priestess.[3]

The *Los Angeles Herald Examiner* of December 21, 1969, commented on the rising tide of Satanism: "Tales of witchcraft cults that sacrifice animals and turn humans into 'slaves of Satan' are coming out of the mountains that form a bucolic backdrop to the Northern California coastal town (of Santa Cruz). Police are paying greater heed to these macabre stories in the aftermath of disclosures about the so-called 'black magic' practices of Charles Manson." The *Herald Examiner* further stated, "Investigators also tell of teenagers who described witchcraft initiation ceremonies in which participants must eat the entrails of an animal while its heart is still beating. There are also numerous reports of persons being placed under hypnotic-type spells by a head witch who slips LSD into ceremonial wine."

Concerned about the slaughter of animals in these rites, the director of the Santa Cruz Animal Shelter commented, "Whoever is doing this is a real expert with a knife. The skin is cut away without even marking the flesh. The really strange thing is that these dogs have been drained of blood." In San Jose, California, Chief of Detectives Barton Collins noted a horrifying application of this technique to *humans*. On August 2, 1969, two young girls were viciously stabbed more than three hundred times, said Collins, "yet there was virtually no trace of blood where the victims' bodies were found."[4]

The *Toronto Daily Star*, September 5, 1970, reported:

[3] Brad Steiger and Warren Smith, *Satan's Assassins* (New York, N.Y.: Lancer Books, Inc.).
[4] *American Opinion*, September, 1970.

In California, two drifters in their early twenties were arrested for murder and cannibalism. One of the accused, Stanley Baker, told police he had been on an acid trip and was hitch-hiking when a motorist picked him up. Baker said he awoke in the car during a storm and was driven into a demonic trance by thunder and lightning. Baker admitted killing the motorist and eating his heart and other portions of the body. His motive: to give worship to the Devil.

In a similar case, banner headlines in the *Los Angeles Times* of July 10, 1970, shook residents of California. One frightening headline read: SATAN WORSHIP TALE UN-FOLDS IN SLAYING CASE. The story told how Steven Hurd, a dedicated worshiper of Satan, and two other "brothers of the shadows" had committed a ritual murder, picking as their victim a thirty-one-year-old female schoolteacher. After brutally murdering her, they cut out the woman's heart, removed her lungs and one arm, whereupon they presented the grisly mess as a sacrifice to the devil. Young Hurd's lawyer stated that his client had been told by the "chief devil," a San Francisco man, that "the devil's cult believes it is all right to 'snuff people out,' providing a portion of the body is used in a sacrifice offering."

The *London Sunday Pictorial*, October 5, 1958, had quite a write-up about Juan Aponte, who was considered a "respected" citizen of Vineland, New Jersey. Aponte was one who used voodoo to obtain sexual power over women. A certain black-sorcery rite called for him to obtain "the skull of an innocent young boy." Aponte was found guilty of killing a thirteen-year-old boy "by striking him a blow upon the back of the head and then strangling him with a cord. . . . He buried the body under the dirt floor in his home. Seven months later he dug up the body, cut off the head, and carefully dried it in a stove. Then he performed a hideous ritual with a lock of hair from the woman he desired, placing it within the skull of the sacrifice." Aponte was examined by six psychiatrists at his preliminary hearing and was found to be perfectly rational and sane.

As one searches out the ways of Satanism, he finds horror piled upon horror. The following UPI report was released in November, 1967: "Two parents practicing black magic dipped their six-year-old son's feet into boiling water every two days during a month of torture, police said. . . . 'When we recovered him, his feet were just globs of raw and bleeding flesh,' said Colonel Palma Cabral. 'The rest of his tiny body had been burned and cut.' "

The parents of this poor child readily confessed that they had tortured and brutalized their own son as part of a "witchcraft ceremony" to the devil. These practicing Satanists were likewise found "sane and rational."

Another tragic case concerns a young farm lad from Iowa who was introduced to drugs, black masses, and Satanism in the Haight-Ashbury area of San Francisco. During weekly LSD trips, he and the group would offer incantations and chants of welcome to demon spirits. He admits, "An evil spirit took control of my body." Stricken with fear, he now believes himself to be a fallen angel. Answering only to the spirit-given name of Raka, he sleeps at night with a tight black satin hood over his head to quiet the "thing" that now possesses him (*Esquire*, March, 1970).

In the October 23rd edition of the *Los Angeles Free Press* appeared the following shocking ad: "CHRIST IS EVIL . . . GIVE YOUR SOUL TO A REAL GOD. ASK FOR HELP AND SATAN WILL HEAR."

All the evidence strongly indicates that the evil tide of Satanism is rising rapidly in many countries. From Agra, India, comes this newspaper story:

> (Reuters, December 30, 1969)—A wealthy landlord sacrificed a fourteen-year-old boy by hacking him to pieces and offering his blood to a goddess in the belief she would make him a million-aire. . . .
>
> Two persons, one a Hindu priest, have been arrested in connection with the alleged sacrifice but the landlord was still being sought, police said. The incident is alleged to have occurred in Kukarson village, near the city of the Taj Mahal. . . .
>
> Police said the landlord dreamed that the goddess, Chavan Devi, would give him a clue to a $2.8 million fortune if he offered the boy as a sacrifice.

At the present time, stately old England is a boiling caldron of witchcraft and black magic activity. Witchcraft and Satanist covens are springing up in the British Isles at an alarming rate. One Church of England spokesman has stated, "We are frightened of what seems to be a steady and continuing growth in the popularity of witchcraft and devil worship." Vast numbers of young people in Britain are being attracted to the dark side of occultism. In the unsettled times in which we live, people are becoming disenchanted with the emptiness of life and are turning on to occultism, hoping to find an ultimate meaning.

In September, 1970, newspapers both in Britain and abroad reported that thirty-five-year-old Michael Harrington hanged himself because he believed his girl friend—a member of one of these black magic cults—had put a curse on him. Commenting on Michael's suicide, Canon Pearce-Higgins stated, "In England today, it is so easy to join one of these cults dedicated to devil worship and practise of evil.

Once a person is trapped in a cult, it is extremely difficult to get out. Suicide is about the only way a member can leave, and we've had a number of them in recent years."

In May, 1970, another youth was charged with murder of an earl's grandson. Next to the victim's body, police found a bloodstained letter containing the words: "Hail Satan!" The letter concluded with the Lord's Prayer written backward. Throughout England, graves have been opened and corpses defiled by roving bands of thrill-seeking Satanists. The Reverend Percey Gray, vicar of St. Crispin's Anglican Church in South London, states that literally scores of graves have been desecrated in his churchyard since January 1970. In one instance, a baby's corpse had been dug up and used for an obscene Satanic ceremony.

Under the pall of darkness, Satanists have broken into English churches, urinating, defecating, and fornicating on church altars. They have stolen sacramental wafers, holy water, church robes, communion chalices, and have wantonly destroyed church property.

In London, a Dominican monk by the name of Dom Petit-Pierre reports, "The devil has deceived people into believing that the practise of black magic is simply a bit of easy fun. They quickly learn that the devil has taken over their lives. Why else would these cultists break into churches and tombs? They dig up graves in the darkness of night and carry out their rituals over rotting corpses." AP quotes police authorities as saying that in London alone there are over a score of black magic groups whose members are "apparently respectable businessmen" who meet to dance naked and perform perverted church services.

Several debates have raged around the subject of black magic in the British House of Parliament. One English law officer who has investigated several grave-robberies makes this statement: "These cultists are frequently men and women who hold respectable positions by day. . . . Many of these people are wealthy. They leave their respectability at home when they venture out into the night. They prowl through the darkness in their devil's uniforms, breaking into graveyards, and holding black masses over some disinterred corpse."

In November, 1963, voices were being raised in Britain to reinstate the laws against witchcraft which had been taken off the statute books in 1951, but Britain's Home Secretary said he "refused to turn back the clock to 1735. . . ." Yet so much havoc and fear are being generated that a member of the House of Commons, Gwilyn Roberts, has again raised the question of black magic in the House: "Many people are losing their minds. They are ending up in mental institutions. There are tremendous dangers in worshiping the devil. The more a person studies the phenomena, the more one realizes that it must be prevented before it is too late. My constituents have plagued me with their pleas for assistance in stopping this growing menace."

12.

Judgment to Come

■ There are two appointments every person must keep. Regardless of how unpleasant the prospect might seem, each one of us will one day be called upon to face death and judgment. Man does not like to talk about death. But whether he likes to admit it or not, man is on a long funeral march from the cradle to the grave.

Death stalks us as his prey at every turn of life's road. None of us knows who will be his next victim. Perhaps it will be *you!* It may not be today or tomorrow, but it is inevitable that somewhere down the road of life, the Grim Reaper will knock upon your heart's door. What is it like to die? What frightening thoughts will you have when the dreaded Death Angel puts forth his icy hand and takes your last breath away? Job of old asks the haunting question: "But man dieth, and wasteth away: yea, man giveth up the ghost, *and where is he?*" (Job 14:10).

The philosophers and sages of every age have tried to understand the riddle of death; human reason reels at its finality. Science and philosophy are speechless before the melancholy silence of a grave site. Death will become to many the dread opener of mysterious doors. The unregenerate man is wise to fear death, because the Bible calls it an enemy. Yet man is born to die.

Life is a sacred trust. God has bestowed upon each one of us conscious existence so that we might enjoy Him forever. The Creator has given us eyes to behold His handiwork so that with adoring wonder we might look up and see Him who made all things. Man has been given an intellect so that he might think his way through to God. We all have a part to play upon the stage of time. This is our day of opportunity; we can either live for selfish pleasures and personal pursuits, or we can spend time and energy serving the God who created us. What will your decision be?

> Choose well; Your choice is
> Brief, and yet endless.[1]

Occult practitioners do not die easy. There are cases on record where black-art traffickers have died in awful agony, and while on their deathbeds they have been known to plead for weeks: "Take the gift from me so I can die!" Not only is this the case with occultists, but God-rejecters and atheists have likewise experienced fearful deathbed scenes.

In the book *Dying Testimonies of Saved and Unsaved* (1898), the Reverend S. B. Shaw relates many well-authenticated deathbed scenes of infidels and atheists. The record states that in those days many unbelievers died in awful agony of soul. They did not have the drugs we have today. Hence dying people of that era were not eased out into eternity like they are today in our modern hospitals. People back there mostly died at home in their own beds *while fully conscious.* Shaw writes about the death of a wealthy farmer, the son of a Methodist preacher:

[1] J. H. Leckie, *The World to Come and Final Destiny* (New York, N.Y.: Chas. Scribner's Sons).

This farmer was highly respected in the community in which he lived. He was a kind-hearted and benevolent man; but, however, had one great fault—he was very profane. He would utter the most horrible oaths without, seemingly, the least provocation. On several occasions, I remember having seen him under deep conviction for salvation during a camp-meeting; he was brought under powerful conviction. He afterwards said he was suddenly frightened, and felt as if he wanted to run away from the place. Just one year from that time, another camp-meeting was held at the same place, and he was again brought under conviction, but refused to yield; after which he was suddenly taken ill, and died in three days. I was with him in his last moments. He seemed to be utterly forsaken of the Lord from the beginning of his sickness. The most powerful medicines had no effect on him whatever. Just as the sun of a beautiful Sabbath morning rose in its splendor over the eastern hills, he died—in horrible agony. All through the night previous to his death, he suffered untold physical and mental torture. He offered the physicians all his earthly possessions if they would save his life. He was stubborn to the very last; and would not acknowledge his fear of death until a few moments before he died; then, suddenly he began to look, then to stare, horribly surprised and frightened, into the vacancy before him; then exclaimed, as if he beheld the king of terrors in all of his merciless wrath, "My God!" The indescribable expression of his countenance, at this juncture, together with the despairing tones in which he uttered these last words, made every heart quake. His wife screamed, and begged a brother to pray for him; but he was so terror-stricken that he rushed out of the room. The dying man continued to stare in dreadful astonishment, his mouth wide open, and his eyes protruding out of their sockets, till at last with an awful groan,

"Death bore the wretch away."

In some cases, the bloodcurdling screams of the lost, while in the throes of death, could be heard blocks away. Infidels have died screaming that they could see devils in the room waiting to drag their lost souls down to hell. So dreadful were some deathbed scenes that relatives fled out of the house and would not return until the screaming man expired! Nurses who have attended some well-known dying infidels have stated that they wish never again to go through such a terrifying ordeal.

There are also present-day testimonies on record of those whose spiritual eyes have been opened to glimpse the spirit world just prior to passing over. Dr. E. D. Hettinger, Pastor of Ebenezer Baptist Church, Plymouth, Pennsylvania, mentions in his sermon "One Hour from Hell" the fearful death of a modern-day twenty-six-year-old business executive. This man's wife pleaded with him to accept Christ. He kept putting the matter off, saying that he would accept the Lord later on in life. Within a few months, he became very ill with an incurable disease and was taken to hospital. For six weeks he suffered terribly both in body and soul. Yet he would not accept Christ. On the last morning of his life, he became very uneasy and fearful. The sick young man seemed to sense that death would soon claim him. He had not been given morphine to deaden his senses, because the doctors had not expected him to die so soon. During his last moments, he bolted up in bed "and stared straight ahead as though seeing into another world. Suddenly his eyes opened wide in anguish, he gave a horrible scream, and fell back dead." The wife is convinced that her unsaved husband at the moment of death saw the very gates of hell itself and knew with an awful certainty that he was going there.[2]

Many of the lost, at the time of death, are so petrified with fear that they are unable to utter any sounds whatever. As

[2] *The Sword of the Lord*, March 24, 1972.

the final night approaches, they stare in dumb amazement at the horror before them. Terror upon terror looms up before their startled gaze, until at last the soul in strangled agony quits its house of clay.

Christ plainly taught this truth when He drew back the veil and showed us what really occurs when the saved and the lost pass over into eternity:

> And it came to pass, that the beggar died, and was carried by the angels into Abraham's bosom: the rich man also died, and was buried; And in hell he lift up his eyes, being in torments. . . . (Luke 16:22–23)

Note that the beggar when he died was taken to paradise, figuratively called 'Abraham's bosom.' He did not get there by himself; he was escorted to paradise by a band of angels. If such is true on the positive side, and remember it is the Lord Jesus telling us these things, then we have every reason to conclude that the lost are likewise escorted down to hell at the time of their death. How else would they get there?

When God withdraws His hand and the wicked expire, then the creatures of evil fly upon their helpless screaming victims and drag them down to hell. What unspeakable, endless torments into which the damned do fall! The Bible declares, "Then said the king to the servants, Bind him hand and foot, and take him away, and cast him into outer darkness; there shall be weeping and gnashing of teeth" (Matt. 22:13).

The Bible teaches that at the time of death, fear will grip the ungodly like a storm. Distress and anguish shall come upon them like a whirlwind (Prov. 1:27). And this is but the beginning of eternity.

Certainly God is love. But the God of the Bible has two

sides to His nature—mercy and justice. At Sinai, God thundered forth His holy commandments. Calvary demonstrated to man the love and mercy of God. The justice of God demands that sin be punished. But the love of God saw the sad plight of lost sinful men and yearned to find a way to redeem man from the awful penalty of sin. Thus God's salvation must not only be able to save man, but it must also fully satisfy all the demands of divine justice.

There was only one who could meet this great need. The angel announced, "Thou shall call his name JESUS: for he shall save his people from their sins" (Matt. 1:21). Out of love for lost humanity, Christ left the glories of heaven to come down into this sin-cursed world. The Innocent One died upon a cruel cross to redeem guilty sinners. He who was rich, for our sakes became poor. He who knew no sin, became sin for us. Never did justice and mercy so triumph, and embrace each other, as when our Savior hung upon a cross.

Sin has left a crimson stain upon the soul of man, but His blood, the blood of God's Son, washes whiter than snow. When men reject or ignore God's great sacrifice for sin, the Lord Jesus Christ, *then they fall victims to the awful wrath of God*. All the fury and terror of Almighty God will be unleashed upon the Christ-rejecting soul.

If it takes the fear of hell to motivate some people toward God, then I'm all for preaching on eternal judgment. As a witness for Christ, I would be remiss in my Christian duty if I did not warn you concerning the awfulness of hell.

Friend, you need not go to hell. We read in Scripture that Christ will be the sinner's refuge and hiding place. Isaiah tells us that a man (the God-man Christ Jesus) "shall be as an hiding place from the wind, and a covert from the tempest" (Isa. 32:2). Those of you who know not Christ, how will you stand in that great day when the thunders of divine judgment

roar and the lightnings of God's anger flash upon sinful men?
What protection will you have when the terrible storm breaks
upon your poor defenseless head? The poet expresses the
awesomeness of judgment to come in these words:

> That day of wrath, that dreadful day,
> When heaven and earth shall pass away,
> What power shall be the sinner's stay?
> How shall he meet that dreadful day?

> When, shrivelling like a parched scroll,
> The flaming heavens together roll;
> When, louder yet, and yet more dread,
> Swells the high trump that wakes the dead,—

> O, on that day, that wrathful day,
> When man to judgment wakes from clay,
> Be thou the trembling sinner's stay,
> Though heaven and earth shall pass away!
> —*Sir Walter Scott*

13.

Power in the Blood

■ The blood of Christ speaks to us concerning the gracious compassion of our Savior Jesus Christ. The Scripture puts it in these words: "[Christ] hath given himself for us an offering and a sacrifice to God for a sweetsmelling savour" (Eph. 5:2). It was not merely a mortal man who hung between heaven and earth that dark dreary day there on Golgotha's brow so long ago. Saint Paul makes careful mention of the fact that it was none other than "the Lord of Glory" whom this wicked world crucified. He who hung on Calvary's cross was both God and man: "Great is the mystery of godliness: God was manifest in the flesh" (I Tim. 3:16).

Out of love for us, heaven gave up its choicest jewel—the Lord Jesus Christ—so that we—poor, weak, failing creatures of dust—might find eternal life. It is only through the mercy, grace, and compassion of heaven's redeeming Lamb of God that man can be saved from the awful penalty of sin. All the far-distant galaxies in the universe, all the myriad stars with their accompanying planets, the total wealth of the universe would not in any way be comparable in value to Christ's *precious blood*. For there is no substance, no action in the uni-

verse that can take away man's sin except the shed blood of
Christ.

> Forasmuch as ye know that ye were not redeemed with corrupti-
> ble things, as silver and gold, from your vain conversation re-
> ceived by tradition from your fathers; But with the precious
> blood of Christ, as of a lamb without blemish and without spot (I
> Pet. 1:18–19)

The cleansing blood of Christ redeems each penitent soul
not only from Satan's grasp, but also from the curse of God's
holy law. The law of the Almighty condemns me to hell because I am a sinner. "The soul that sinneth, it shall die," is
the divine decree (Ezek. 18:4). The law of God justly condemns me, but Christ has satisfied all the claims of divine
justice by dying in my stead: "For he hath made him [Christ]
to be sin for us, who knew no sin; that we might be made the
righteousness of God in him" (II Cor. 5:21).

Such wondrous love, that One so holy should die for such
a wretch as me! Now we are beginning to see why evil principalities and powers, demons, and hellish archfiends hate
the blood of Christ. The avowed purpose of the hierarchy of
evil is to mislead, deceive, and damn men to hell. However,
since Christ defeated Satan and his fallen cohorts at Calvary,
their intention to plunge all mankind into the same state of
awful spiritual chaos and ruin as they are in has been
thwarted. A way of escape and deliverance has been made
possible. This is the reason demonic spirits react so violently
whenever someone, quickened by God's Holy Spirit, makes
mention of the redeeming power of Christ's blood. Those
who involve themselves in spiritualism and other occult activities would do well to heed the following admonition of
Scripture:

Beloved, believe not every spirit, but try the spirits whether they are of God. . . . Hereby know ye the Spirit of God: Every spirit that confesseth that Jesus Christ is come in the flesh is of God: And every spirit that confesseth not that Jesus Christ is come in the flesh is not of God: and this is the spirit of antichrist. (I John 4:1–2)

What does the Scripture mean here when it speaks of confessing "that Jesus Christ is come in the flesh?" To confess this great truth means to believe everything the Bible tells us about Christ. It means we must believe that Jesus Christ is the virgin-born Son of God, the only Savior of sinners, the One who was crucified and then buried, the One who rose bodily from the dead on the third day, the One who was truly God manifested in the flesh, whose blood alone can cleanse from sin.

THE FIRST BLOOD SACRIFICE

In Eden's garden, Almighty God inaugurated the first blood sacrifice. You will recall that when Adam and Eve sinned, they hid themselves from "the voice of the Lord God walking in the garden in the cool of the day." A cloud overshadowed them that awful day, as they stood and listened with frightened interest to an angry God pronouncing the anathema upon the serpent: "I will put enmity between thee and the woman, and between thy seed and her seed; it shall bruise thy head, and thou shalt bruise his heel" (Gen. 3:15).

In this portion of Scripture, we have the first promise of a Redeemer, a Man-Child, Christ the Lord, who would one day come through woman and bruise the serpent's head. The head is the central area of all intelligent life, whereas the heel is but a lesser part of the body. This prophecy suggests to us that one day Satan's seat of power—the serpent's head—would be bruised and finally crushed, but the heel of Emmanuel's power, which still is upon the serpent's head, would be wounded. This took place when Christ hung upon the cross for the sins of lost men.

In the Garden of Eden, Adam, in fear and trembling, answered the insistent voice of God, saying, "I heard thy voice in the garden, and I was afraid, because I was naked; and I hid myself" (Gen. 3:10). Divine judgment was then pronounced against Adam and Eve and all their offspring. Yet the account goes on to say that the justice was tempered with mercy.

There is another truth here that should be made known. The Bible tells us, "Unto Adam also and to his wife did the Lord make coats of skins, and clothed them" (Gen. 3:21). The text indicates that God shed blood to obtain coats of skins for Adam and Eve. The blood spilled for our first parents' disobedience acted as a temporary covering for their sin, until the Lamb of God would come and give His blood, which would not merely cover sin, but take it away.

What has just been said is further supported by the incident of Cain and Abel. These two brothers presented their respective offerings to the Lord one day. Abel gave an animal sacrifice to God, and it was accepted. Cain, however, did not bring a blood sacrifice; instead, he presented "the fruit of the ground" unto the Lord. It was rejected. Why? Because the fruit of the ground represented the toil and labor of his own hands; whereas, Abel's offering, the animal sacrifice, had a substitutionary and vicarious significance.

The Passover

The Egyptians greatly oppressed the Israelites, and made their lives so miserable and bitter with hard bondage, that the children of Israel cried unto God for deliverance. God heard their pitiful cries and sent His servant Moses to warn Pharaoh that he must release God's people.

The king of Egypt insolently replied, "Who is the Lord, that I should obey his voice to let Israel go? I know not the Lord, neither will I let Israel go" (Exod. 5:2). Consequently, God chastised Pharaoh for his insolence and stubbornness by sending a variety of plagues upon Egypt. In spite of these stern warnings of divine judgment, Pharaoh remained obstinate and refused to obey God's command.

The heart of Pharaoh became hard as the nether millstone. He was resolved on the matter—stubborn as iron sinew—so the Lord directed Moses to announce yet one more plague, a plague that would make every heart sad and every house a scene of dire mourning. Scripture says, "There shall be a great cry throughout all the land of Egypt, such as there was none like it, nor shall be like it any more." It was the destruction of the firstborn of every man and beast.

The divine executioner would put his invisible hand to the sword and go throughout Egypt destroying all the firstborn, from the son of the haughty king who sits on his throne to the son of the lowest slave toiling at Pharaoh's mill, even to the very sheep bleating in the fields. Who can stay the mighty hand of God once His vengeance is unleashed? Let proud Egypt assemble her troops; let Pharaoh set his soldiers to guard every house. It will not do any good! The sword of Jehovah's anger is unsheathed and will pierce through Pharaoh's legions as lightning penetrates the air.

Moses feared the awful visitation of God's judgment that was to fall on Egypt, and he was concerned lest some of his own people might be cut down. What precautions could he possibly take for their safety?

The Lord ordered Moses to slay a lamb. The head of each Israelite family was to do likewise, and to receive the blood of their sacrificial lamb into a basin, then sprinkle it on the lintels and sideposts of their doors. The blood of the lamb would be a sign to the destroying angel, who would pass over every house thus marked.

The children of Israel had God's promise: "And the blood shall be to you for a token upon the houses where ye are: and when I see the blood, I will pass over you" (Exod. 12:13). With the lamb's blood on their doorposts, they had no cause to be "afraid for the terror by night; nor for the arrow that flieth by day; Nor for the pestilence that walketh in darkness; nor for the destruction that wasteth at noonday" (Ps. 91:5–6).

The Day of Atonement

As the nation of Israel began to mature, a priesthood was set up. On the Day of Atonement, which was celebrated annually, the high priest offered two expiatory sin offerings, one for himself and the other for his people. He entered the Holy of Holies, once for himself and then on behalf of the people, and sprinkled sacrificial blood seven times upon the mercy seat, and seven times before it.

Upon the brow of every high priest in Israel was a golden miter that bore the inscription, "Holiness to the Lord," typifying that perfect holiness was an absolute prerequisite in one acting as mediator between God and man. Symbolically, this told every Jew that the coming Messiah would possess holiness. His action in sprinkling the blood symbolized that the Lamb of God would shed His blood for the remission of men's sins.

THE LAMB OF GOD

The teaching of Scripture makes it abundantly clear that Christ is both God and man. We may not intellectually understand it; nevertheless, this divine truth is reiterated time and again in God's Word. One of the texts used to support Christ's deity is John 1:1: "In the beginning was the Word, and the Word was with God, and the Word was God." Not only was the eternal Word, or Logos, God, but as John says, "And the Word was made flesh, and dwelt among us" (John 1:14).

Consider, if you will, the implications of such scriptural statements. The Almighty Son of the Living God has taken upon himself man's nature! Here is a truth whose depths are beyond sounding. When the eternal God became man, He suffered more than any mortal man could possibly suffer. We would be greatly humiliated if the whole human race were turned into burrowing worms of the dust, but to have the glorious universal Monarch of the Spheres stoop down and take a garment of human flesh for His covering—*this is humiliation!* He that is "more excellent than the angels" condescended to become lower than the angels *for the suffering of death.* "He that thought it not robbery to be equal with God, was made in the likeness of man." He came in lowliness, that man might be set free.

Yea, His August Majesty of the celestial realms became the contempt of sinners and shame of men. Isaiah reflects the humiliation of the Messiah in these words: "He is despised and rejected of men; a man of sorrows, and acquainted with grief: and we hid as it were our faces from him; he was despised, and we esteemed him not" (Isa. 53:3).

What a contrast! That the Lord of Glory and the shame of men should come together. Who can measure the greatness of our God? His ways are past finding out. To think that He suffered such abasement to save us from the righteous anger of Heaven's offended holiness! Here is a love beyond compare! Well saith the apostle Paul, "He made himself of no reputation" (Phil. 2:7).

From the day of our Lord's birth to the time of His death, rejection was His constant companion. When He was a babe in Bethlehem, there was no room for Him at the inn. Let His poor cradle be a smelly manger—it is good enough, says man, for the Creator! John tells us, "He came unto his own, and his own received him not" (John 1:11).

Christ's mission to our world is summed up in these words: "For God sent not his Son into the world to condemn the world; but that the world through him might be saved" (John 3:17). He came so that we might have life and have it more abundantly. Christ came to redeem man from the lostness into which he had plunged himself.

> For it is not possible that the blood of bulls and of goats should take away sins. Wherefore when he cometh into the world, he saith, Sacrifice and offering thou wouldest not, but a body hast thou prepared me: In burnt offerings and sacrifices for sin thou hast had no pleasure. Then said I, Lo, I come (in the volume of the book it is written of me,) to do thy will, O God. (Heb. 10:4-7)

How could men reject Him? They were blinded by their own sinful pride and prejudices. Hence they stumbled on like ungrateful brutes in the darkness of their own selfish ways.

We now come to the deepest part of our Lord's descent and His greatest rejection. Christ was making ready to give Himself as an offering for sin. He took the disciples and went to the Garden of Gethsemane. Upon their arrival, Christ said to the disciples, "Sit ye here, while I go and pray yonder" (Matt. 26:36). The Bible tells us that Jesus unburdened this thought to them: "My soul is exceeding sorrowful, even unto death" (Matt. 26:38). Jesus prayed three times to His Father saying, "Father, if thou be willing, remove this cup from me: nevertheless not my will, but thine, be done" (Luke 22:42).

The sorrow and anguish in our Savior's soul there at Gethsemane would have all but crushed Him if an angel had not been sent to strengthen Him. Theologians usually make a distinction here between Christ's natural will and what is often referred to as a "rational will." The natural will of Jesus recoiled and trembled at the pangs of death. Yet in His "rational will," our Lord was willing to drink that bitter cup. Thomas Aquinas said that a man will not naturally endure the lancing of any member of his body; yet in his "rational will" he gives consent to it, if mutilation is for the good of the whole body. Reason takes precedence over sense of pain, if the cutting, cauterizing, or amputation thus endured will save the body. Thus we see that in His natural will, Christ feared death, but His reason perceived that the crucifixion of His mortal body would bring eternal life to the Church, our Lord's spiritual body.

Many of our Lord's followers have endured fearsome physical torments culminating in slow, agonizing death. Yet it was with noble courage that they faced "the tyrant's brandished steel and the lion's gory mane." Did He who gave His followers divine courage to face the Pale Monarch quake at death? No! What Christ feared in the garden that night no other man has ever felt. The Holy Spirit expresses our Lord's great anguish in these heart-rending words:

Who in the days of his flesh, when he had offered up prayers and supplications with strong crying and tears unto him that was able to save him from death, and was heard in that *he feared;* Though he were a Son, yet learned he obedience by the things which he suffered; And being made perfect, he became the author of eternal salvation unto all them that obey him. (Heb. 5:7–9)

Our Savior knew he was to suffer the pangs of hell for every member of the human race. All the sins and iniquities of every person born into our world were to be laid on Him; until He was pressed, "as a cart is pressed that is full of sheaves" (Amos 2:13). And when every man's sin was mystically placed upon the bleeding, bruised, and tortured body of the sinless Son of God, He had then to be prepared to bear the awful pressure of divine judgment against the sins of the living, the dead, and the yet unborn. This is why our blessed Savior was so alarmed, why He was so very much afraid and trembled exceedingly.

The Psalmist catches something of our Savior's feelings in Gethsemane when he utters these words: "Thy terrors have I suffered with a troubled mind." The heaviness of such a thought drew from Him those tears of blood and anguish. Holy Writ tells us, "And being in an agony He prayed more earnestly, and His sweat was as it were great drops of blood falling down to the ground."

The great depths of our Savior's soul were broken up when this deluge of grief, high as mountains and deep as seas, rolled with relentless fury over Him. It was for a lost world that Christ endured such an unutterable woe. Christ saw our everlasting destruction; He saw the terrors that He must suffer to save us. Christ could have avoided the cup of grief, but out of love for us, He willingly gave His life to ransom lost sinners.

Upon finishing His prayer, our Lord was seized in the garden by an unruly mob stirred up by the chief priests and Pharisees. It is written that they came against Him with swords and staves, but He retaliated with just a verbal encounter—"I am He." The power inherent in the divine "I Am" of Exodus 3:14 resulted in their being thrown backward on the ground. If our Lord had desired, He could have ordered fire from heaven to consume them, or commanded the earth to open and swallow them up. Christ could even have called down shafts of lightning from heaven and burned every last one of them to cinders. More than twelve legions of angels were at His beck and command, and any angel was well able to destroy all the legions of Rome. Yet our Lord granted them permission to take Him, power to kill the holy Son of God.

The Crucifixion

The main part of our Lord's redemption was now about to take place. The ax of death was ready to cut down His manhood. They extended the hands of Jesus and fastened them to a cross, soldiers driving nails through those hands which healed so many. Every thud of the weighty hammer brought forth spurts of blood.

Now the feet of Jesus, that carried God's heart in a temple of flesh over Israel's dusty roads, had nails driven through them. He that hath ears to hear the hammer blows, let him hear.

But it was not cruel nails that held Jesus to the cross. It was His great love for us. By a mere word of power He could have dissolved those ugly nails and taken away their tearing pain. Yet Jesus willingly endured the nails of death so that "through death he might destroy him that had the power of death, that is, the devil" (Heb. 2:14).

Hardened soldiers lifted the cross from the ground and dropped it into a hole. At the moment of impact, Christ's flesh and sinews were ripped and torn. Speaking prophetically of Christ, the Psalmist says, "All my bones are out of joint" (Ps. 22:14).

Up on the cross, Jesus was left to bleed, suffer, and die. It was twelve o'clock, high noon, and the sun was in its zenith, but being unable to endure the woeful sight of nature's Creator being put to death, Phoebus went into mourning and refused to show his face. "Now from the sixth hour [noon] there was darkness over all the land unto the ninth hour" (Matt. 27:45).

The whole of inanimate creation groaned in sympathy that day as its Maker was dying on a cross—sun, earth, rocks and sepulchers, all were thrown into convulsions by the awful deed. The only part of creation insensitive to the bleeding and suffering of Christ was man. Man had placed upon Christ's head a crown of thorns that raked and harrowed His blessed brow until blood ran down His face: "His visage was so marred more than any man" (Isa. 52:14).

His hands were crucified for us to show that the works of men's hands were unacceptable to a holy God. The feet of Jesus were crucified to show that man's walk in life is displeasing to God. His face was polluted with the vile spittle of sinful men; His ears were assaulted with the taunts and scoffs of blasphemy; yea, the stench of man's sin covered Christ as He hung upon the blood-stained cross.

All the sins and sorrows of a lost world came flooding in upon His soul. His hair was clotted with blood from the cruel crown of thorns. His face, shoulders, and breast were all covered with blood. It was not just ordinary blood flowing that day at Calvary. *It was holy blood!*

In the strange darkness of that afternoon, all the awful

vials of God's angry wrath were emptied upon the gory, mangled, and bloody form of Christ. Hanging upon the cross, Christ cried out, "My God, my God! why hast thou forsaken me?" The disciples had all left Him. Angels hid their heads in shame underneath weeping wings. But the deepest loneliness our Lord felt was during the fleeting moment when He believed that the Father had forsaken Him.

It may seem strange to us that the Eternal Father would turn His back upon Christ during such a time of awful suffering. Howbeit, divine holiness demands that the Father veil His Presence from the Son while He is being made a sin offering. This thought of the veiled presence of God is suggested in Habakkuk 1:13: "Thou art of purer eyes than to behold evil, and *canst not look on iniquity*."

The holiness of God can have no fellowship with sin. While Christ was taking upon Himself the sins of the world, His fellowship with heaven and the Father was severed. Christ hung on the cross, friendless and alone among His enemies. The Jews, imperial Rome, and all hell were against Him. Our Lord's cup of suffering was full to the brim, and He was dying, dying for the sins of humanity—for you and me.

Finally, the bleeding Savior cried out in a loud voice, "IT IS FINISHED!" The Lamb of God had been sacrificed—a full, perfect, and sufficient sacrifice for the whole world.

Calvary is God's meeting place with man. It is a place soaked with the blood of God's holy Son. This is why evil spirits both fear and hate the blood of Christ. At the cross, not only was man's redemption secured, but Satan's power was broken forever! Scripture puts it in these words: "And having spoiled principalities and powers, he made a shew of them openly, triumphing over them" (Col. 2:15).

CHRIST'S DESCENT INTO HELL

When Christ died, He went down into hades (Acts 2:31). There appear to be several reasons why Christ at His death made a visit to the infernal regions. One reason was to seize the keys of death and hell from Satan. Another reason was that He might preach unto the spirits in prison (I Pet. 3:19). These spirits referred to here as being "in prison" are confined to the abyss or Tartarus, which is the lowest hell. Bound by chains of darkness, these fallen angels are under irrevocable judgment (Jude 6; II Pet. 2:4). Christ's message was not one of grace and hope, but rather an announcement of His victory over Satan. (The Greek word for "preach" in this context suggests a royal messenger announcing an official proclamation.)

The Scripture does not explain in detail all that happened when Jesus descended into hell. Human language has not adequate power to describe the awful scene when our Lord entered the dreaded domain of devils and encountered the thrones, princedoms, powers, and dominions of the infernal realm.

Fully aware of our inadequacy, let us nevertheless try to faintly picture what it must have been like when the Lord of Glory descended those dark winding labyrinths which led ever downward to the gates of hell. He who was the brightness of the Father's glory, and the express image of His Person, entered that terrifying realm where Chaos and Terror ruled as chief monarchs. His divine Presence illuminated those eternal shadows, breaking the bands of darkness and death.

The brightness of our Lord's glory must have sent demon sentries howling through hell's corridors. All hell was stirred by the presence of heaven's Lord of Light. From the thrones of night, black-winged messengers were dispatched to mobilize all of hell's forces. Legions of infernal spirits readied themselves to do battle with the Lord from heaven.

In the vanguard of hell's armies came a legion of writhing, serpentlike demons, hissing forth streams of fiery venom against man's deliverer. He who is the Lord, mighty in battle, scattered them with a Word. Infernal intelligence then summoned the fiery, blasting winds of hell against Him, but the Master of the elements stilled the howling rage of hell's subterranean winds.

As our Lord continued His journey through the infernal regions, another menace loomed forth with dire threatenings. Great black slimy shapes arose from the brackish pits, and out of the yawning mouths of these bellowing creatures came a vomiting black stream full of deadly purulence. The God-man but raised His hand of authority, and the ugly hellish things went squealing and squirming back to the sulfurous ooze from whence they came. Heaven's Warrior then made His way through the dank Stygian marshlands of hades, when suddenly a chill mist of horrors, wide as the wasteful deep, overshadowed Him. Armed with omnipotence, our Lord sheared hell's poisonous mist, chained its suffocating tentacles, and walked through to the other side.

Nothing could deter the Lion of Judah from issuing His proclamation of victory over sin and death to the High Council of Hell. As man's Savior continued on His determined course, He had to pass by the black caves of hell. At His approach, the whole terrifying landscape—earth, rocks, and burning fissures—begin to quake and tremble. Cries of yelling monsters and damned souls rent the tortured air. All hell trembled at the presence of this monarch from on high.

Scurrying up from the wild abysms of this dreaded place appeared the startled, gaping fiends of darkness, who swarmed unnumbered like a plague of destroying locusts. Yet they were unable to move against man's Savior; for a holy power encircled these fearsome creatures, striking them with paralysis. Yea, they were welded into immobility and forced to remain perched upon the black fiery crags of hell. Incensed with indignation and rage, they could only gawk in angry silence as Jesus passed by.

Passing hell's bottomless deeps, the Mighty One approached the infernal city with its red glowing walls. Emblazoned upon the gates of hell was the harsh Dantean inscription etched in letters of fire:

> Through me you pass into the city of woe:
> Through me you pass into eternal pain:
> Through me among the people lost for aye.
> Justice the founder of my fabric moved:
> To rear me was the task of power divine,
> Supremest wisdom, and primeval love.
> Before me things create were none, save things
> Eternal, and eternal I endure.
> All hope abandon, ye who enter here.[1]

Standing before the massive gates, Jesus raised His voice, full of thundering omnipotence:

> Lift up your heads, O ye gates; and be ye lift up, ye everlasting doors; and the King of glory shall come in. (Ps. 24:7)

Above the gates of hell were gathered all the chief captains and chancellors of this doleful realm. Baring their grinning fangs, they howled forth in maddened tones a bestial reply: "Who is it that dares to invade the domain of devils?" That voice full of authority and power answered:

---

[1] Dante's *Inferno*, tr. by Henry F. Cary (New York, N.Y.: The Colonial Press, 1971).

Who is this King of glory? The Lord strong and mighty, the Lord mighty in battle. Lift up your heads, O ye gates; even lift them up, ye everlasting doors; and the King of glory shall come in. Who is this King of glory? The Lord of hosts, he is the King of glory. (Ps. 24:8–10)

Unable to resist the radiance, glory, and authority of heaven's Holy One, all the evil hosts of darkness capitulated. Christ smashed the gates open[2] and continued His downward descent to the very citadel of ultimate evil—Satan's throne room. Infernal spirits in wild confusion cried forth, "Behold the Harrower of Hell approaches!"

The mighty Conqueror entered the inner sanctum of Satan's lair and officially declared His victory over sin and death. Satan and all his arch-minions were in attendance, obscenely squatting upon the black thrones of night. The whole infernal hierarchy was forced to concede that they had been conquered by heaven's Prince of Light. He who is Monarch of the Spheres had defeated them by robing Himself in a garment of dust and dying for sinful men. These impious rebels cried out in great alarm, *"Thou hast vanquished us!"*

Behold our Lord as He now walks upon the broken crowns and smashed scepters of demon princes. See heaven's conquering King take the keys of death and hell out of Satan's cruel hand. The seat of all Satanic authority is now broken and left in disarray amidst awful ruin.

It is true that the dark forces are still able to wield some influence and power. But let it be known that Satan and his underlings now have only *delegated authority*. Since their defeat at Calvary, God has granted the devil and his demons special

---

[2] On Holy Saturday in the Roman Catholic Church, the Mass is sung in these words: "Hodie portas mortis et seras pariter Salvator noster disrupit" (On this day our Savior broke open the door of the dead and its lock as well).

permission to tempt and test mankind. Thus they serve God's purpose by revealing who can resist the allurements and enticements of sin. For it is one thing to say that one loves God, but it's something else again to prove it by resisting evil.

When Christ seized from Satan the keys of death and hell, He left the dark domain of devils and crossed that impassable great chasm which separates the wicked dead from the departed righteous. Hades was divided into two sections. One part of hades was a place of torment where the wicked go at death. The other section of hades was a place of comfort and hope. This is where all the Old Testament saints went at death. It was not possible for the righteous who had died prior to Christ to ascend into heaven, because Christ's blood had not yet been shed for man's sin. Therefore they had to wait until Christ came for them. Many Bible scholars refer to them as "prisoners of hope." They get this from Isaiah 14:17, where it is written that Satan "did not let his prisoners go home" (RSV).

Another one of the reasons Christ descended into hell was to loose these prisoners and take them home to glory. "When he [Christ] ascended on high, he led a host of captives . . ." (RSV).

These Old Testament saints are trophies of our Savior's redeeming grace; they are the first fruits of the redeemed. What rejoicing there must have been when Christ ascended into heaven bringing His sheaves with Him! The Psalmist catches a prophetic glimpse of this joyous occasion: "God is gone up with a shout, the Lord with the sound of a trumpet" (Ps. 47:5). What a shout that must have been! A shout of joy and of triumph! Our Savior had just won the battle of the ages. He had destroyed Satan's power (Heb. 2:14). By His death, Jesus spoiled evil principalities and powers and made an open show of them (Col. 2:15). Hallelujah! The Lord met man's greatest enemy—death—broke his horrid jaws and took his keys away. Death was stripped of his dreaded power and could no longer wave his black banner in triumph over God's people. For Jesus defeated him by rising from the dead a mighty conqueror. The grave could not hold Him; neither could hell keep its prey. And because He lives, we who believe on the Son of God shall also live.

God has granted man great powers. He can search out the ways of truth and become what God intended him to be—an heir of heaven with irrevocable citizenship in the glorious world to come. Or, if man so desires, he can plumb the depths of spiritual wickedness and become allied with demons. God gives unto every man a free choice in the matter. The prophet of Jehovah long ago cried out, "Choose you this day whom ye will serve" (Josh. 24:15).

We are asked by the Almighty to make a personal decision. The whole matter is plainly stated in these challenging words: "I have set before thee this day life and good, and death and evil" (Deut. 30:15). God permits man, if he so chooses, to actually follow the road of death and evil. Each one of us, then, has been granted a free choice: we can live for God and do good to our fellow creatures, or we can wreak havoc and evil in the world. It is up to each individual what decision he makes. God will not transgress upon the sovereignty of man's free will. But there is a day coming "when God shall judge the secrets of men by Jesus Christ" (Rom. 2:16).

In this book we have set before you good and evil, life and death. What is done with the truth presented in these pages is entirely up to the reader. Light rejected bringeth night. The decision you make regarding what has been said here will determine your eternal destiny. Even now Christ stands at the door of your heart knocking. Won't you accept Him today as your Lord and Savior? Regardless of your past life, Jesus extends to you this gracious invitation:

> Come unto me, all ye that labour and are heavy laden, and I will give you rest. Take my yoke upon you, and learn of me; for I am meek and lowly in heart: and ye shall find rest unto your souls. (Matt. 11:28–29)